Mistaken Identity

Mistaken Identity

Race and Class in the Age of Trump

Asad Haider

VERSO

First published by Verso 2018
© Asad Haider 2018

The moral rights of the author have been asserted

1 3 5 7 9 10 8 6 4 2

Verso
UK: 6 Meard Street, London W1F 0EG
US: 20 Jay Street, Suite 1010, Brooklyn, NY 11201
versobooks.com

Verso is the imprint of New Left Books

ISBN-13: 978-1-78663-737-6
ISBN-13: 978-1-78663-739-0 (UK EBK)
ISBN-13: 978-1-78663-738-3 (US EBK)

British Library Cataloguing in Publication Data
A catalogue record for this book is available from the British Library

Library of Congress Cataloging-in-Publication Data

Names: Haider, Asad, author.
Title: Mistaken identity : race and class in the age of Trump / Asad Haider.
Description: London ; Brooklyn, NY : Verso, 2018. | Includes bibliographical
  references.
Identifiers: LCCN 2017051520| ISBN 1786637375 (pbk.) | ISBN 9781786637390 (UK
  EBK) | ISBN 9781786637383 (US EBK)
Subjects: LCSH: Political culture—United States. | Identity politics—United
  States. | United States—Race relations—Political aspects. | African
  Americans—Politics and government. | Whites—United States—Politics and
  government. | United States—Social conditions—21st century.
Classification: LCC JK1726 .H35 2018 | DDC 306.20973—dc23
LC record available at https://lccn.loc.gov/2017051520

Typeset in Sabon by Biblichor Ltd, Edinburgh
Printed and bound by CPI Group (UK) Ltd, Croydon, CR0 4YY

Contents

Acknowledgments

I first have to thank Chris Connery, who encouraged me to write this book, who was the first reader of the completed manuscript, and who pushed me to make it come together as a whole, and Ben Mabie, who is responsible for giving this idea a concrete form in his capacity as publishing impresario and editor. Both were also valued interlocutors in the formation of the ideas this book presents.

Indeed, these ideas were produced collectively along with friends, comrades, and colleagues. I cannot possibly mention them all, but I hope they all recognize my enormous gratitude. I will mention here those who discussed these questions with me in the whirlwind of political practice, those who encouraged me to record my thoughts and helped me to make them comprehensible, and those who valiantly read and commented on the entire draft: Robert Cavooris, Deborah Gould, Erin Gray, Evan Grupsmith, David Lau, Patrick King, Wendell Hassan Marsh, Dave Mesing, G.S. Sahota, Jason Smith, Alberto Toscano, Delio Vasquez, Gavin Walker, and Philip Wohlstetter.

My adventures in publishing began with an intellectual and political collaboration with Salar Mohandesi, whose influence is present throughout this book. Along the way I have come to collaborate with the entire *Viewpoint* collective, and all of them have been valued readers, critics, and interlocutors.

The historical details of the manuscript were reviewed by Emma Teitelman, Tim Barker, and Matt Karp, whose encouragement I greatly appreciated. Sarah Grey's precise and perceptive copy editing gave the text an indispensable refinement. Any remaining errors are my own responsibility.

I have probably not had a single idea in my life that was not formed in some kind of dialogue with my brother, Shuja Haider. He has emerged as one of the most significant critics of identity politics today; if I have not cited him in this book, it is only to avoid confusing readers.

Without the constant personal support of Julie McIntyre, I would never have produced anything. She is also the source of far more intellectual stimulation and inspiration than she is willing to admit. I am eagerly looking forward to her first book.

I dedicate this book to my parents, Jawaid Haider and Talat Azhar, who taught me never to compromise on ethical principles, even if they go against the prevailing wisdom and incur the wrath of the authorities.

Introduction

We all have to be born somewhere, wrote the philosopher Louis Althusser. I was born in a small town in Central Pennsylvania, though it was hard to figure out why. No one could pronounce my name, and at home we spoke another language; and every other summer we packed up and spent long, excruciating hours in airplanes to see our extended family in Karachi.

I'm not so sure I emerged from this experience with anything resembling an identity. Whatever bits and parts may have constituted my selfhood appeared to be scattered all over the globe. Identity, paradoxically, appeared to be externally determined—or perhaps more saliently, not determined. Between the white kids in Pennsylvania who asked me where I was from (not Pennsylvania, apparently) and the Pakistani relatives who pointed out my American accent, it seemed that if I did have an identity, no one was really prepared to recognize it.

But I suppose I came to experience my identity differently in September of 2001. One day I arrived at school and learned that the country had been attacked, and for the rest of the day we watched planes crashing into the World Trade Center, over and over. I had trouble parsing the reactions of my classmates. Understandably, they were horrified, angry, devastated. I was puzzled.

It wasn't unusual to see reports of terrorist incidents, military actions, and even coups in Pakistan on TV. I remember a newscaster solemnly intoning that Karachi was "the most violent city in the world." In my childhood summers there, I had seen the streets filled with children like me, who were homeless, starving, too weak to bat the flies off their bodies.

Something in the political geometry was out of alignment, and the view from Pennsylvania seemed inordinately narrow. When Bill Clinton ordered a missile attack on the Al-Shifa pharmaceutical plant in Sudan, my sixth-grade teacher had us sit down and write a paragraph explaining why such an act was necessary. But I knew that on the other side of the television screen there was a mass of human beings who saw things differently.

The collapse of the Twin Towers, which we watched with disbelief, also reverberated in my everyday experience. Until then, I had learned to live with a culture of condescending and exclusionary toleration. But now it revealed an undercurrent of open hostility. I found myself being called "Osama" by my classmates while the teacher watched with either apathy or agreement. I was seized with unexpected fear at the ice-cream shop when an avuncular old white man suddenly scowled at the sight of my family and began ranting in our direction about "terrorists from Iraq," as we made our way to a table, threateningly wielding cones of cookies-and-cream.

My identity had become a matter of homeland security. But how could I respond to such a scenario? Should I proudly claim a fixed Pakistani identity, one that never felt quite like the right fit, that belonged to a place on the other side of the world? Or should I assimilate into the world of whiteness around me, even though it was racist and parochial and had never really welcomed me?

If there was an answer to these questions, it was not supplied at school. So, alongside my other readings—most memorably the *Communist Manifesto* and *Tropic of Cancer*—I began to study the question of identity. But this was not in order to adopt an identity. Between Marx and Engels's "Workers of the world, unite!" and Henry Miller's nomadism—in which, as Gilles Deleuze put it, "everything is departure, becoming, passage, leap, daemon, relationship with the outside"—I was convinced of the impossibility of settling on fixed territory.[1]

In sixth grade, I did a science project on Newton's three laws of motion. Next to Isaac Newton in the biography section of the public library was "Newton, Huey P." It was an impressive-looking book with a disorienting title: *Revolutionary Suicide*. His story spoke to me. In this very country, in this white, alienating world, there were others who had lived through the experience of exclusion, indeed, far worse than anything I had ever experienced. I read with horror Newton's account of solitary confinement in prison but was moved by his commitment to learning to read by repeatedly working his way through Plato's *Republic*. He joined his intellectual development to his political practice as founder of the Black Panther Party, and this set for me a model of the life of the mind that was far more convincing than the bohemian hedonism of Henry Miller or the self-serving social climbing expected of members of a "model minority."

But what mattered the most to me was that Newton did not stop with his own identity. His experience led him beyond himself—to take up a politics based on solidarity with Cuba, China, Palestine, and Vietnam. His example corroborated the *Communist Manifesto*: the vast poverty I had witnessed in Pakistan and the long history of racial oppression that echoed into present-day Pennsylvania went hand in hand. Any solution would have to confront them both. The insights of this brilliant thinker, Karl Marx, did not belong to Europe. They belonged to the whole world, to everyone who fought against injustice. They had been refined and developed in Asia, Africa, and Latin America. Even here in the belly of the beast, amid the acid and bile of patriotism and evangelicalism, black Americans had shown that this legacy could not be geographically confined.

I read *The Autobiography of Malcolm X* afterward and approached it with greater ambivalence, skeptical as I had become of all forms of religion. Even in the face of anti-Muslim discrimination, some of it targeted specifically at me, I was never tempted to defend Islam. I hated the religious fanatics who had gotten the rest of us into this mess; I hated the whole culture of irrationalism, mythology, and sexual shame. But it was part of me nonetheless, in words, sounds, music, architecture, and it brought Malcolm closer to the world I knew. Islam, for him, had served as a path beyond fanaticism; it had led him past his fixation on his own identity and toward a solidarity with the whole world. As he said at Oxford University in 1964: "I for one will join in with anyone, I don't care what color you are, as long as you want to change this miserable condition that exists on this earth." Against the rise of anti-Muslim sentiment, expressed even by supposed leftists who railed on about "Islamo-fascism," this was the kind of Muslim I could be proud to be associated with.

But there was no real solution to the double bind they had put me in, the Muslims and the whites. Was it possible to respond to the attacks on Muslims without rationalizing the conservative and reactionary ideology of Islam? On the other hand, was it possible to criticize the damage wrought by Islamic fundamentalism without playing into the hands of white racists?

The work of Hanif Kureishi, a British Pakistani novelist who dared to cast his lot with the bohemian subcultures that emerged from London punk, was a revelation. His film *My Son the Fanatic,* based on his own short story, addressed these questions in a way I had never seen in American culture. A young British Pakistani boy named Farid tires of studying to be an accountant and dumps the white fiancée whose traditionalist English parents had so much trouble tolerating him. Suddenly and unexpectedly, he becomes a fundamentalist Muslim—much to the surprise of his father, Parvez, a cab driver who is much more interested in listening to Louis Armstrong than the prophet Muhammad. Farid convinces his father to allow a mullah visiting from Lahore to stay in their house. The mullah spends the morning watching

Western cartoons and eventually asks Parvez for help getting a visa so he can live in the Western civilization he decries so loudly.

The discovery that others felt as adrift as I did—some of them even Pakistani, though they seemed to be mostly located in England—was both a shock and a relief. In an introduction to the screenplay for *My Son the Fanatic*, Kureishi addresses the double bind that we shared:

> Fundamentalism provides security. For the fundamentalist, as for all reactionaries, everything has been decided. Truth has been agreed and nothing must change. For serene liberals, on the other hand, the consolations of knowing seem less satisfying than the pleasures of puzzlement, and of wanting to discover for oneself. But the feeling that one cannot know everything, that there will always be maddening and live questions about who one is and how it is possible to make a life with other people who don't accept one, can be devastating. Perhaps it is only for so long that one can live with that kind of puzzlement. Rationalists have always underestimated the need people have for belief. Enlightenment values—rationalism, tolerance, skepticism—don't get you through a dreadful night, they don't provide the spiritual comfort or community or solidarity.[2]

Enlightenment values are often good ideas, and those of us who read a lot of books are often hopeful that we can change the world with them. I was no exception. I read Noam Chomsky obsessively, arming myself with facts and principles, and dove headfirst into the movement against the Iraq War, a movement which mushroomed at the nearby college campus when I was a sophomore in high school. This political rationalism offered a certain kind of comfort. It confirmed that I did not have to rely on my identity to argue that the solution to the violence and suffering that assaulted us in our daily news was an end to American imperialism, and therefore global capitalism.

Over the years, however, I have learned how badly this rationalism can fail. As Kureishi observes, it is devastating to live with questions about who you are; it is also devastating to confront a world in which so much is wrong and unjust. To oppose this injustice, the project of universal emancipation, of a global, revolutionary solidarity, can only be realized through organization and action. I believe it is possible to achieve this, to carry forward the struggle of those who came before. But the dominant ideology is hard at work convincing us that there is no alternative. In this flat, hopeless reality, some choose the consolations of fundamentalism. But others choose the consolations of identity.

1

Identity Politics

In 1977, the term *identity politics* in its contemporary form was introduced into political discourse by the Combahee River Collective (CRC), a group of black lesbian militants that had formed in Boston three years earlier. In their influential collective text "A Black Feminist Statement," founding members Barbara Smith, Beverly Smith, and Demita Frazier argued that the project of revolutionary socialism had been undermined by racism and sexism in the movement. They wrote:

> We are socialists because we believe that work must be organized for the collective benefit of those who do the work and create the products, and not for the profit of the bosses. Material resources must be equally distributed among those who create these resources. We are not convinced, however, that a socialist revolution that is not also a feminist and anti-racist revolution will guarantee our liberation.

The statement brilliantly demonstrated that "the major systems of oppression are interlocking" and proclaimed the necessity of articulating "the real class situation of persons who are not merely raceless, sexless workers."[1] Black women, whose specific social position had been neglected by both the black liberation movement and the women's liberation movement, could challenge this kind of empty class reductionism simply by asserting their own autonomous politics. As a way of conceptualizing this important aspect of their political practice, the CRC presented the hypothesis that the most radical politics emerged from placing their own experience at the center of their analysis and rooting their politics in their own particular identities:

> This focusing upon our own oppression is embodied in the concept of identity politics. We believe that the most profound and potentially most radical politics come directly out of our own identity, as opposed to working to end somebody else's oppression.[2]

Now this did not mean, for the CRC, that politics should be reduced to the specific identities of the individuals engaged in it. As Barbara Smith has recently reflected:

> What we were saying is that we have a right as people who are not just female, who are not solely Black, who are not just lesbians, who are not just working class, or workers—that we are people who embody all of these identities, and we have a right to build and define political theory and practice based upon that reality ... That's what we meant by identity politics. We didn't mean that if you're not the same as us, you're nothing. We were not saying that we didn't care about anybody who wasn't exactly like us.[3]

Indeed, the CRC demonstrated this perspective in its actual political practice. Demita Frazier recalls the emphasis the organization placed on coalitions:

> I never believed that Combahee, or other Black feminist groups I have participated in, should focus only on issues of concern for us as Black women, or that, as lesbian/bisexual women, we should only focus on lesbian issues. It's really important to note that Combahee was instrumental in founding a local battered women's shelter. We worked in coalition with community activists, women and men, lesbians and straight folks. We were very active in the reproductive rights

movement, even though, at the time, most of us were lesbians. We found ourselves involved in coalition with the labor movement because we believed in the importance of supporting other groups even if the individuals in that group weren't all feminist. We understood that coalition building was crucial to our own survival.[4]

For the CRC, feminist political practice meant, for example, walking picket lines during strikes in the building trades during the 1970s. But the history that followed seemed to turn the whole thing upside down. As Salar Mohandesi writes, "What began as a promise to push beyond some of socialism's limitations to build a richer, more diverse and inclusive socialist politics" ended up "exploited by those with politics diametrically opposed to those of the CRC."[5] The most recent and most striking example was the presidential campaign of Hillary Clinton, which adopted the language of "intersectionality" and "privilege" and used identity politics to combat the emergence of a left-wing challenge in the Democratic Party surrounding Bernie Sanders. Sanders's supporters were condemned as "Bernie Bros," despite his widespread support among women; they were accused of neglecting the concerns of black people, despite the devastating effect for many black Americans of the Democratic mainstream's commitment to neoliberal policies. As Michelle Alexander wrote in the *Nation*, the legacy of the Clinton family was a Democratic capitulation "to the right-wing backlash against the civil-rights movement" and "Ronald Reagan's agenda on race, crime, welfare, and taxes." The new brand of Clinton liberalism ended up "ultimately doing more harm to black communities than Reagan ever did."[6]

The communications director of Clinton's campaign, Jennifer Palmieri, said during an MSNBC interview about the anti-Trump protests following the inauguration, "You are wrong to look at these crowds and think that means everyone wants fifteen dollars an hour. Don't assume that the answer to big crowds is moving policy to the left . . . It's all about identity on our side now."

To be fair, Palmieri is not solely to blame for this error in judgment. In fact, she was really just expressing a classical and inescapable tenet of liberalism. Judith Butler has explained that "identities are formed within contemporary political arrangements in relation to certain requirements of the liberal state." In liberal political discourse, power relations are equated with the law, but as Michel Foucault demonstrated, they are actually produced and exercised in a range of social practices: the division of labor in the factory, the spatial organization of the classroom, and, of course, the disciplinary procedures of the prison. In these institutions, collectivities of people are separated into individuals who are subordinated to a dominating power. But this "individualization" also constitutes them as political subjects—the basic political unit of liberalism, after all, is the individual. Within this framework, Butler argues, "the assertion of rights and claims to entitlement can only be made on the basis of a singular and injured identity."[7]

The word *subject*, Butler points out, has a peculiar double meaning: it means having agency, being able to exert power, but also being subordinated, under the control of an external power. The liberal form of politics is one in which we become *subjects* who participate in politics through our *subjection* to power. So Butler suggests that "what we call identity politics is produced by a state which can only allocate recognition and rights to subjects totalized by the particularity that constitutes their plaintiff status." If we can claim to be somehow injured on the basis of our identity, as though presenting a grievance in a court of law, we can demand recognition from the state on that basis—and since identities are the condition of liberal politics, they become more and more totalizing and reductive. Our political agency through identity is exactly what locks us into the state, what ensures our continued subjection. The pressing task, then, as Butler puts it, is to come up with ways of "refusing the type of individuality correlated with the disciplinary apparatus of the modern state."[8]

But we can't possibly achieve this if we take these forms of individuality for granted—if we accept them as the starting point of our analysis and our politics. Clearly "identity" is a real phenomenon: it corresponds to the way the state parcels us out into individuals, and the way we form our selfhood in response to a wide range of social relations. But it is nevertheless an abstraction, one that doesn't tell us about the specific social relations that have constituted it. A materialist mode of investigation has to go from the abstract to the concrete—it has to bring this abstraction back to earth by moving through all the historical specificities and material relations that have put it in our heads.

In order to do that, we have to reject "identity" as a foundation for thinking about identity politics. For this reason, I don't accept the Holy Trinity of "race, gender, and class" as identity categories. This idea of the Holy Spirit of Identity, which takes three consubstantial divine forms, has no place in materialist analysis. Race, gender, and class name entirely different social relations, and they themselves are abstractions that have to be explained in terms of specific material histories.

For precisely that reason, this book is entirely focused on race. That is partly because my own personal experience has forced me to think of race beyond the easy theological abstraction of identity. But it is also because the hypotheses presented here are based on research into the history of race, racism, and antiracist movements. Of course, studying any concrete history necessarily requires us to deal with all the relations constitutive of it, and thus we will encounter the effects of gender relations and movements against gender-related oppression. But I make no claim to offer a comprehensive analysis of gender as such; to do so would require a distinct course of research, and to simply treat gender as a subsidiary question to race would be entirely unacceptable. There is already much work along these lines to consider. Butler's *Gender Trouble* is itself one of the most prescient and profound critiques of identity politics as it exists within the specific discourse of feminist theory. In Butler's own words, her critique "brings into question the foundationalist frame in which feminism as an identity politics has been articulated. The internal paradox of this foundationalism is that it presumes, fixes, and constrains the very 'subjects' that it hopes to represent and liberate."[9] But here I focus on race, and I will be primarily concerned with the history of black movements, not only because I believe these movements have fundamentally shaped the political parameters of our current historical moment, but because the figures to whom these movements gave rise are at the apex of thinking on the concept of race. There is also the matter of my personal contact with black revolutionary theory, which first exposed me to Malcolm X and Huey Newton's critiques of the precursors of identity politics. Following their practice, I define identity politics as the *neutralization* of movements against racial oppression. It is the ideology that emerged to appropriate this emancipatory legacy in service of the advancement of political and economic elites. In order to theorize and criticize it, it is necessary to apply the framework of the black revolutionary struggle, including the Combahee River Collective itself. These movements should not be considered deviations from a universal, but rather the basis for unsettling the category of identity and criticizing the contemporary forms of identity politics—a phenomenon whose specific historical form the black revolutionary struggle could not have predicted or anticipated, but whose precursors it identified and opposed.

Malcolm's analysis was cut short in 1965 when he was assassinated by the cultural nationalists of the Nation of Islam, with whom he had broken after connecting with revolutionary anticolonial movements in Africa and Asia, which he constantly invoked in his speeches. He had deepened his structural analysis of white supremacy and the economic system on which it rested. As Ferruccio Gambino has demonstrated, this is not surprising when we look at Malcolm's life as a laborer—as a Pullman porter and a final assembler at the Ford Wayne Assembly Plant, where he encountered the tension between the workers' antagonism toward the employer and the restraint imposed by the union bureaucracies.[10] "It's impossible for a white person to believe in capitalism and not believe in racism," Malcolm said in a 1964 discussion. "You can't have capitalism without racism. And if you find one and you happen to get that person into conversation and they have a philosophy that makes you sure they don't have this racism in their outlook, usually they're socialists or their political philosophy is socialism."[11]

The Black Panther Party followed through on Malcolm's growing practice of revolutionary solidarity and his critique of the Nation of Islam's cultural nationalism, which they called "pork-chop nationalism." The pork-chop nationalists, Huey Newton argued in a 1968 interview, were "concerned with returning to the old African culture and thereby regaining their identity and freedom," but ultimately erased the political and economic contradictions within the black community. The inevitable result of pork-chop nationalism was a figure like "Papa Doc" Duvalier, who used racial and cultural identity as the ideological support for his brutally repressive and corrupt dictatorship of Haiti. Newton argued that it was necessary to draw a "line of demarcation" between this kind of nationalism and the kind that the Panthers espoused:

> There are two kinds of nationalism, revolutionary nationalism and reactionary nationalism. Revolutionary nationalism is first dependent upon a people's revolution with the end goal

being the people in power. Therefore to be a revolutionary nationalist you would by necessity have to be a socialist. If you are a reactionary nationalist you are not a socialist and your end goal is the oppression of the people.[12]

Another leader of the Black Panther Party, Kathleen Cleaver, has reflected on how the revolutionary nationalism of the Panthers led them to understand the revolutionary struggle as a specifically cross-racial one:

> In a world of racist polarization, we sought solidarity ... We organized the Rainbow Coalition, pulled together our allies, including not only the Puerto Rican Young Lords, the youth gang called Black P. Stone Rangers, the Chicano Brown Berets, and the Asian I Wor Kuen (Red Guards), but also the predominantly white Peace and Freedom Party and the Appalachian Young Patriots Party. We posed not only a theoretical but a practical challenge to the way our world was organized. And we were men and women working together.[13]

That's an obvious conclusion when you understand socialism the way Huey Newton did: as "the people in power." It can't be reduced to the redistribution of wealth or the defense of the welfare state—socialism is defined in terms of the political power of the people as such. So not only is socialism an indispensable component of the black struggle against white supremacy, the anticapitalist struggle has to incorporate the struggle for black self-determination. Any doubt about this, Newton pointed out, could be dispelled by studying American history and seeing that the two structures were inextricably linked:

> The Black Panther Party is a revolutionary nationalist group and we see a major contradiction between capitalism in this country and our interests. We realize that this country became

very rich upon slavery and that slavery is capitalism in the extreme. We have two evils to fight, capitalism and racism. We must destroy both racism and capitalism.[14]

This was not, however, a new insight of the Black Panthers. While I was growing up, the civil rights movement had been rendered palatable for mainstream audiences, and I had sought out the more militant-seeming legacy of Black Power. But thanks to the work of scholars and activists who have practiced fidelity to the revolutionary content of the civil rights movement, it is becoming evident that recognition for an injured identity cannot possibly describe this movement's scope and aspirations. Nikhil Pal Singh writes in his important book *Black Is a Country* that the reigning narrative of the civil rights movement "fails to recognize the historical depth and heterogeneity of black struggles against racism, narrowing the political scope of black agency and reinforcing a formal, legalistic view of black equality."[15]

As the historian Jacquelyn Dowd Hall elaborates in her analysis of the "long civil rights movement," Martin Luther King Jr. has been rendered an empty symbol, "frozen in 1963." Through selective quotation, Hall observes, the uplifting rhetoric of his speeches has been stripped of its content: his opposition to the Vietnam War, through an analysis linking segregation to imperialism; his democratic socialist commitment to unionization; his orchestration of the Poor People's Campaign; and his support for a sanitation workers' strike when he was assassinated in Memphis.[16]

When we move past the misleading and restrictive dominant narrative, it becomes clear that the civil rights movement was in fact the closest US equivalent to the mass workers' movements in postwar Europe. Those European movements structured the revolutionary project and the development of Marxist theory.[17] But the development of such a movement was blocked in the United States—and, as we will see, many militants came to the conclusion that the primary obstacle to its development was white supremacy.

However, what makes a movement anticapitalist is not always the issue it mobilizes around. What is more important is whether it is able to draw in a wide spectrum of the masses and enable their self-organization, seeking to build a society in which people govern themselves and control their own lives, a possibility that is fundamentally blocked by capitalism. So the black freedom struggle is what most closely approached a socialist movement—as the Trinidadian intellectual and militant C.L.R. James put it, the movements for black self-determination were "independent struggles" that represented the self-mobilization and self-organization of the masses and were thus at the leading edge of any socialist project.[18] Autoworker and labor organizer James Boggs took this argument even further, suggesting in *The American Revolution*:

> At this point in American history when the labor movement is on the decline, the Negro movement is on the upsurge. The fact has to be faced that since 1955 the development and momentum of the Negro struggle have made the Negroes the one revolutionary force dominating the American scene ... The goal of the classless society is precisely what has been and is today at the heart of the Negro struggle. It is the Negroes who represent the revolutionary struggle for a classless society.[19]

There were also direct connections to a specifically anticapitalist history, because in the 1930s the Communist Party (CP) had trained many of the organizers and established many of the organizational networks that became part of the civil rights movement. As Robin D.G. Kelley, whose book *Hammer and Hoe* is a major history of the Communist Party USA's antiracist work, has put it, the CP helped lay "the infrastructure that ... becomes the Civil Rights Movement in Alabama."[20]

Rosa Parks, for example, got involved in politics through the Communist-organized defense of the "Scottsboro Boys," nine black teenagers falsely accused in Alabama of raping two white women and convicted by an all-white jury. In the 1940s, a coalition of black radicals and union leaders, including figures who played a major role in the 1960s like A. Philip Randolph, formed a "civil rights unionism." Jacquelyn Dowd Hall points out that their actions were founded on "the assumption that, from the founding of the Republic, racism has been bound up with economic exploitation." In response, civil rights unionists carried out a political program in which "protection from discrimination" was matched with "universalistic social welfare policies." Their demands encompassed not only workplace democracy, union wages, and fair and full employment but also affordable housing, political enfranchisement, educational equity, and universal healthcare.[21]

This was the first phase of the civil rights movement. As the movement developed into its most famous, "classical" period, it responded to changing circumstances and confronted strategic and organizational limits. Racial oppression was tied up not only with legal segregation but also with the organization of urban space, hierarchies of political representation, the violence of the repressive state apparatus, and economic exclusion and marginalization.[22] The extraordinary victories of the 1950s and 1960s civil rights mobilizations, the 1964 Civil Rights Act and the 1965 Voting Rights Act, did not transform these fundamental structures. After 1965, mass mobilizations would have to incorporate different strategies and different demands, and the languages of Black Power and black nationalism responded to this need.

The earlier struggles had always been complex and variegated, going beyond the now celebrated nonviolent protests of the South. Armed resistance had played a vital role in enabling the use of nonviolent tactics, and movements in the North ran parallel to their equivalents below the Mason-Dixon line. But organizations like the NAACP, led by the elites of the black community, had tried to distance themselves from the revolutionary possibilities of the struggle, shifting funding and resources away from economic issues and toward the battle against Southern legal segregation. As time went on, this became a significant limit on the scope of mass mobilization.

But throughout the 1960s, the epicenter of the struggle began to shift to the urban rebellions of the Northern inner cities, which broke forcefully outside this bureaucratic containment. The movement was in search of new forms of self-organization that could overcome the obstacles the Civil Rights Act and the Voting Rights Act had been unable to address, and black nationalism provided a promising approach. What nationalism meant was a political perspective: black activists organizing themselves rather than following the lead of white organizations, building new institutions instead of seeking entry into white society.

The contradiction of the nationalist mobilizations, however, came in the form of what Huey Newton described as "reactionary nationalism," represented by groups like Ron Karenga's US Organization, with which the Panthers would later violently clash. As Newton pointed out, reactionary nationalism put forth an ideology of racial identity, but it was also based on a material phenomenon. Desegregation had made it possible for black businessmen and politicians to enter into the American power structure on a scale that had not been possible before, and these elites were able to use racial solidarity as a means of covering up their class positions. If they claimed to represent a unitary racial community with a unified interest, they could suppress the demands of black working people whose interests were, in reality, entirely different from theirs.

So the Black Panther Party had to navigate between two concerns. They recognized that black people had been oppressed on a specifically racial basis, and so they had to organize autonomously. But at the same time, if you talked about racism without talking about capitalism, you weren't talking about getting power in the hands of the people. You were setting up a situation in which the white cop would be replaced by a black cop. For the Panthers, this was not liberation.

But that was clearly the situation we were getting into in the United States, as optimistic liberals celebrated the replacement of mass movements, riots, and armed cells with a placid multiculturalism. Over the course of several decades, the legacy of antiracist movements was channeled toward the economic and political advancement of individuals like Barack Obama and Bill Cosby who would go on to lead the attack against social movements and marginalized communities. Keeanga-Yamahtta Taylor calls attention to this phenomenon in *From #BlackLivesMatter to Black Liberation*: "The most significant transformation in all of Black life over the last fifty years has been the emergence of a Black elite, bolstered by the Black political class, that has been responsible for administering cuts and managing meager budgets on the backs of Black constituents."[23]

Of course, the existence of elites within the black community was not new in itself. Despite their differences, both the entrepreneurialism of Booker T. Washington and the "Talented Tenth" of W.E.B. Du Bois were early investments in the political potential of the black elite. However, as Taylor recounts, the ensuing history of American politics and the development of the black freedom struggle have transformed the structural role of the black elite. As she points out in an analysis of the murder of Freddie Gray and the ensuing uprising in Baltimore, we have broken in a fundamental way from the context that produced the classical vocabulary of the antiracist struggle:

There have always been class differences among African Americans, but this is the first time those class differences have been expressed in the form of a minority of Blacks wielding significant political power and authority over the majority of Black lives. This raises critical questions about the role of the Black elite in the continuing freedom struggle— and about what side are they on. This is not an overstatement. When a Black mayor, governing a largely Black city, aids in the mobilization of a military unit led by a Black woman to suppress a Black rebellion, we are in a new period of the Black freedom struggle.[24]

Within the academy and within social movements, no serious challenge arose against the cooptation of the antiracist legacy. Intellectuals and activists allowed politics to be reduced to the policing of our language, to the questionable satisfaction of provoking white guilt, while the institutional structures of racial and economic oppression persisted. As James Boggs reflected in 1993,

> Before the Civil Rights Act of 1964 we may have had the money but we couldn't go into most hotels or buy a home outside the ghetto. Today the only reason why we can't go to a hotel or buy a decent home is because we don't have the money. But we are still focused on the question of race and it is paralyzing us.[25]

Making sense of this bewildering history requires us to draw a line of demarcation between the emancipatory mass movements of the past, which struggled against racism, and the contemporary ideologies of identity, which are attached to the politics of a multiracial elite. The existence of this problem is widely recognized, but discussing it constructively has turned out to be quite difficult. Criticisms of identity politics are often voiced by white men who remain blissfully ignorant or apathetic about the experiences of others. They are also, at times, used on the left to dismiss any political demand that does not align with what is considered to be a purely "economic" program—the very problem that the Combahee River Collective had set out to address.

However, here the term *identity politics* seems to amplify the difficulties. Often contemporary radicals are reluctant to criticize even the most elitist expressions of racial ideology, because doing so seems to be dismissing any movement against racism and sexism. Others valiantly attempt to establish a gradient of identity politics, as though there is a minimum effective dose and problems arise only when it is taken to extremes. But this logic of the gradient cannot possibly explain the emergence of fundamentally opposed and antagonistic political positions: the revolutionary grassroots politics of the CRC versus the ruling-class politics of the Democratic Party elite.

It is the haziness of our contemporary category of identity that has blurred the boundaries. Its political pitfalls have been forcefully demonstrated by Wendy Brown, who argues that "what we have come to call identity politics is partly dependent upon the demise of a critique of capitalism and of bourgeois cultural and economic values." When identity claims are put forth without a grounding in a critique of capitalism, Brown suggests,

> identity politics concerned with race, sexuality, and gender will appear not as a supplement to class politics, not as an expansion of left categories of oppression and emancipation, not as an enriching augmentation of progressive formulations of power and persons—all of which they also are—but as tethered to a formulation of justice that reinscribes a bourgeois (masculinist) ideal as its measure.[26]

In other words, by coding demands that come from marginal or subordinate groups as identity politics, the white male identity is enshrined with the status of the neutral, general, and universal. We know that this is false—in fact, there is a white identity politics, a white nationalism—and, as we shall see, whiteness is the prototypical form of racial ideology itself. Antiracist struggles like those of the CRC reveal the false universality of this hegemonic identity.

However, when identity claims lose their grounding in mass movements, the bourgeois masculinist ideal rushes to fill the void. This ideal, Brown writes, "signifies educational and vocational opportunity, upward mobility, relative protection against arbitrary violence, and reward in proportion to effort." If it is not questioned, people of color, along with other oppressed groups, have no choice but to articulate their political demands in terms of inclusion in the bourgeois masculinist ideal.

To demand inclusion in the structure of society as it is means forfeiting the possibility of structural change. As Brown points out, this means that the enabling condition of politics is the "renaturalization of capitalism that can be said to have marked progressive discourse since the 1970s."[27] It is the equation of political agency with membership in a mythical "middle class," which is supposed to characterize everyone in American society. The middle class itself, Brown argues, is "a conservative identity," one that refers to "a phantasmic past, an imagined idyllic, unfettered, and uncorrupted historical moment (implicitly located around 1955) when life was good." This was a historical moment ideologically centered on the nuclear family, with the white male breadwinner at its head. Yet it paradoxically comes to embody, Brown points out, "the ideal to which nonclass identities refer for proof of their exclusion or injury."

Of course, the injury of exclusion from the benefits extended to the white heterosexual middle class is a real injury. Job security, freedom from harassment, access to housing—all of these are meaningful demands. But the problem is that "politicized identities" do not pose these demands in the context of an insurgency from below. The very structure of the politicized identity is to make a demand for restitution and inclusion; as Brown points out, "Without recourse to the white masculine middle-class ideal, politicized identities would forfeit a good deal of their claims to injury and exclusion, their claims to the political significance of their difference."[28]

I grew up in a world entirely shaped by this renaturalization of capitalism. I sensed that there was something unsatisfactory about politicized identity but could not quite find a way to deal with it, beyond a sort of weak dialectical ambivalence. After all, I couldn't possibly dismiss the fact that while "black faces in high places" might not mean liberation, seeing them was still profoundly meaningful for those who had suffered the psychological traumas of a racist society. In my formative years, everyone I saw on TV who looked like me was a cab driver or an Arab terrorist. (I still don't understand why they have Indians play Arab terrorists. Why not at least a Pakistani terrorist?) Every president had been white and, despite my lack of interest in Obama, his electoral victory made me think of the black people who had died fighting for *just the right to vote*; the thought moved me to tears. Was the multicultural bourgeoisie with its ideology of identity a necessary evil—a component of the cross-class alliance that would be required to fight racism?

At times, I thought so. But as I continued to participate in social movements, I was forced to change my mind. By launching a critique of identity politics, then, I have no intention of deviating from the legacy of the Combahee River Collective or the mass movements against racism that have shaped our contemporary world. It is, rather, an attempt to deal with the contradictory reality that we cannot avoid confronting.

In its contemporary ideological form, rather than its initial form as a theorization of a revolutionary political practice, identity politics is an individualist method. It is based on the individual's demand for recognition, and it takes that individual's identity as its starting point. It takes this identity for granted and suppresses the fact that all identities are socially constructed. And because all of us necessarily have an identity that is different from everyone else's, it undermines the possibility of collective self-organization. The framework of identity reduces politics to who you are as an individual and to gaining recognition as an individual, rather than your membership in a collectivity and the collective struggle against an oppressive social structure. As a result, identity politics paradoxically ends up reinforcing the very norms it set out to criticize.

While this redefinition may seem drastic, this kind of shift in meaning is typical of political language, which does not always clearly align with political practice. A word like *nationalism*, for example, ends up revealing irreconcilable divisions. It eventually requires modification, and we may end up deciding that it has to be abandoned in favor of new and more adequate terms. Indeed, nationalism was precisely the epistemological obstacle that drove Barbara Smith to the kind of politics that would frame the CRC. She recalled:

> I went to a major antiwar mobilization in Washington, D.C., in the fall of 1969 ... I thought it was the last demonstration I'd ever go to; one of the reasons being black people back at Pitt had so many nasty things to say about the fact that I was involved in what they say was a "white" entity, namely, the antiwar movement ... it was a very hard time to be a politically active black woman, who did not want to be a pawn ... I actually imagined that I would never be politically active again because nationalism and patriarchal attitudes within black organizing was *so* strong.[29]

The CRC's initiating purpose was precisely to overcome these degrading and depoliticizing divisions. "I firmly believe there has to be space for us all in our myriad identities and dimensions," Demita Frazier would later reflect. "You run the risk of having an identity become crystallized and contained and requiring everyone to be conformists." This tension also existed within the CRC. Class differences internal to the group were a challenge in maintaining democratic forms of organization, Frazier recalls:

> Class was another huge issue that we looked at and yet in some way could not come to grips with. We had an analysis based on our own socialist leanings and a socialist democratic view of the world, and yet, when it came right down to it, we had many women who felt excluded because they felt they didn't have the educational background and privilege of the leadership.

Just as significant was the question of relating to other groups, especially other feminist groups. The women's liberation movement had been perceived as white from the outset, and part of the purpose of the CRC was to insist that black women could articulate their own feminism. But this did not necessarily mean maintaining rigid divisions from white feminists, or indeed forming a crystallized black identity. In Frazier's own words:

> One of the things that has always troubled me is that I wanted to be part of a multicultural feminist organization, a multicultural feminist movement, and I never felt that the feminist movement became fully integrated . . . It isn't that Combahee didn't work in coalition with other groups, but we weren't able to make those linkages across culture and make them as firm as I hoped they could be.[30]

The problem of coalitions is felt acutely by anyone who has experienced the trials and tribulations of political practice. My own experiences with the rise and fall of coalitions convinced me of the perspective of the scholar of black British culture Paul Gilroy: "Action against racial hierarchies can proceed more effectively when it has been purged of any lingering respect for the idea of 'race.'"[31]

2

Contradictions Among the People

On February 15, 2003, 10 to 15 million people in more than 600 cities took to the streets to protest the US invasion of Iraq—the largest protest in human history. I was one of them. My first experiences as an activist were within the painfully small cluster of people organizing against the Iraq War in State College, Pennsylvania. In this group, race was not a source of antagonism. Black anti-imperialists and white anti-imperialists worked together to organize demonstrations; the white activists, some of them radicalized by learning about Mumia Abu-Jamal, argued fervently that racism at home was related to imperialism abroad. We were too small to have any splits.

By the time the Occupy movement rolled around, I had moved to Northern California, where the left is big enough to accommodate a great many splits. What was incredible about this moment was that class came onto the agenda in a way it hadn't before during my lifetime. I came into contact with many more Marxists, and sometimes found myself arguing with the white ones who thought that anti-imperialism and even antiracism were outmoded. The antiwar movement had failed, they insisted, and was full of sectarians who supported Third World autocracies. Antiracism was little more than a slogan, because the real problems of people of color could be explained by the contradictions of the economic base.

I couldn't relate to this and couldn't really see what it had to do with Marxism. I had not encountered anything to convince me to reject Newton's definition of socialism as "the people in power," and it seemed to me that when people organized themselves to resist imperialist and racist oppression, they were working toward building that power, even if the uncertainties of history meant that their efforts often fell short. For some time, I was mainly preoccupied with arguing that the left should take race more seriously.

I thought, in fact, that race was the primary limitation of the Occupy movement. Despite initiatives like Occupy the Hood, the movement of the 99 percent never seemed to take hold in the poorest neighborhoods and never managed to diversify its ranks adequately. As a consequence, it was represented by the corporate media as a white-dominated movement with white-oriented demands. This was an unacceptable propaganda defeat. Not only had black people been deeply, even disproportionately hurt by predatory lending and the consequences of the recession, we also had the black revolutionary legacy to draw upon. It should have been possible to move across the boundaries of race, neighborhoods, and institutions to confront the status quo with a multiracial mass movement.

This didn't happen, and eventually the Occupy movement faded away. But the problem of race came back, like a return of the repressed. In 2014 we saw exactly how ineffectual liberal multiculturalism had been. Despite having a black family in the White House, police violence against the black community had not stopped. When a young black man named Michael Brown was lynched by an unrepentant white police officer, an explosion of discontent rose up in Ferguson, Missouri, and spread to Atlanta, Chicago, Philadelphia, New York, and Oakland.

It was not only the persistence of white supremacy that was exposed in this moment. Just as apparent were the class contradictions of the black community. While black political elites like Al Sharpton urged restraint, the uprisings pointed to demands that went beyond making space for black people in the American dream of social mobility. Black youth continued to be sent to prison or murdered by police, and black communities were kept in states of unconscionable poverty; the rebels on the street saw clearly that collaborating with Sharpton or Obama would not advance their struggle. These contradictions and tensions would only accelerate as time went on, incorporating outrage at the similar case of Eric Garner in New York and coalescing into the movement recognizable as Black Lives Matter.

This movement carried forward a fundamental revolutionary legacy, one that Malcolm X had described in his monumental speech "Message to the Grassroots." His famous analysis of the "house Negro" was not merely a rhetorical response to individuals who tended toward liberal compromise. It was a complex analysis of the structural role played by black leadership and its suppression of autonomous mass action. "They control you," Malcolm said. "They contain you; they have kept you on the plantation."[1] As Cornel West pointed out, the Ferguson uprising was a new revolt against control and containment by these black elites:

> The emergence of Black Lives Matter momentum is a marvelous new militancy that is the early signs of the shattering of the neoliberal sleepwalking in Black America. This emergence exposes the spiritual rot and moral cowardice of too much of Black leadership—political, intellectual and religious. The myopic careerism and chronic narcissism that prevented any serious critique of Obama's neoliberalism are now out in the open, owing to the courageous young people who stood in the face of military tanks in order to show their love of those shot down by unaccountable police under a Black president, Black attorney general and Black homeland security cabinet member.[2]

So the Black Lives Matter movement came from the grassroots. Accordingly, it did not draw an artificial boundary between class and race. As Erin Gray wrote in her analysis of this "revolutionary 21st century anti-lynching movement": "The direct actions organized by the outraged in defense of black life have become increasingly anticapitalist—they have included the destruction of property, freeway occupations, gas station and police department blockades, and shutdowns to major corporations like Walmart."[3]

But although we were seeing the self-mobilization of demographics that the Occupy movement had not managed to reach, this nascent class content was not always easy to maintain and develop. In fact, a reactionary tendency emerged, nourished by the corporate media and the black elite, which tried to introduce a rigid barrier between the Black Lives Matter movement and ongoing anticapitalist struggles, since they supposedly corresponded to different and unrelated identities.

I encountered this problem, in a way I was not prepared for, at the University of California at Santa Cruz, where the Black Lives Matter movement emerged in the context of an antiprivatization movement led by a student-labor coalition. In the few years immediately following Occupy, a range of labor unions—organizing everyone from healthcare workers to bus drivers to custodians to teaching assistants—had gone through contract negotiations and shut down the campus during highly disruptive strikes. They relied on support from student activists, including multiracial leftist groups, like Autonomous Students, but also community groups, like the Movimiento Estudiantil Chicano de Aztlán (popularly known as MEChA).

Of course, groups like the latter had come out of the nationalist upsurge of the 1960s, which had a powerful effect in California, especially in institutions of higher education—the ethnic studies departments at San Francisco State and Berkeley, for example, were established thanks to the student strikes of the Third World Liberation Front.

But this legacy would turn out to be a contradictory one when the University of California (UC) Board of Regents announced a 27 percent tuition hike in November 2014. I hadn't expected much; I was sitting in my office grading, planning to make a quick appearance at the rally on the way home. Then I heard the crowd outside: the building next door had been occupied, the administration ejected. Change of plans.

The occupation lasted about a week, punctuated with visits by Cornel West, Chris Hedges, and the Teamsters. After an initial burst of inchoate energy, conversations finally had to start—the analysis had to be hashed out, slogans printed onto fliers. It was remarkable how, at all of these actions, the race question already dominated everything. It seemed to be most effective, in terms of rallying troops, to say that rising tuition "hits students of color the hardest."

But there was no elaboration, or even argument, for this claim. In fact, when taken in the context of the university's policies around minority admissions, it may not have been the case at all. There may have been reasons for claiming that students of color who grew up in economically segregated neighborhoods and went to similarly segregated public schools were most severely affected by the overall trends of privatization which tuition hikes represent, despite the fact that the poorest among them don't pay tuition. But the insistence that the tuition hikes themselves must be somehow racially biased obscured the complicated mathematics underlying the UC's policy vacillations, and forced the movement into a rhetorical corner—as though racially equitable university privatization would be somehow acceptable.

Alongside this fundamental lack of clarity sat the flabber-gasting opposition to the very words *occupy* or *occupation*, which could have recalled self-managed factories in Argentina and Uruguay but instead were accused of celebrating the geno-cide of Indigenous people. In a stunning reversal of earlier academic fads, the signifier *occupy* was restricted to a single meaning traced back to Christopher Columbus, any suggestion of polysemy rejected as if it were a personal insult. A debate that should probably have happened in a semiotics seminar took up hours at meetings where we could have planned teach-ins and rallies and workshops or allocated cleanup tasks. Instead, we had to pore over the activist thesaurus in search of synonyms like *takeover* or *seizure*.

But things got worse. It started with a debate over authoritarian practices at a disorganized general assembly. The crowd, the biggest yet, was full of excited newcomers who were ready to join in. But they were totally silenced, reduced to receiving instructions that had not been democratically discussed. Many people spoke up to criticize this practice, including me. But each of the facilitators was a "POC"—that's "person of color"—and after the assembly completely unraveled, an almost hilariously unsubstantiated rumor began to spread that the facilitators had been attacked by racists. This rumor became nearly impossible to dispel; even some of the usual supporters heard that the occupation wasn't a "safe space" and stopped showing up.

Of course, it isn't as though these grievances came out of nowhere. Since before the word *microaggression* became part of the popular lexicon, I experienced precisely such forms of subtle racism and the racial paranoia they cultivate. But universities have fostered a depoliticized discourse around these problems, as Combahee member Barbara Smith observed in a recent interview: "Unfortunately because identity politics often have been first introduced to younger people by academics who have a partial understanding of what the depths of it would be, they are also confused about it too. Trigger warnings and safe spaces and microaggressions—those are all real, but the thing is, that's not what we were focused upon."[4]

But this had become the focus in Santa Cruz. Some people began to organize separatist POC meetings, united by their complexion against a fictional collection of white anarchists. My skin got me in the door. After listening to a bewildering array of political positions—one student read aloud an email from an administrator that conspiratorially accused student protesters of attempting to undermine campus diversity initiatives—I felt the need to intervene. I stood and tried to summon up some rhetorical demons the best I could; I thought about Malcolm X, and how he always spoke in the second person ("You don't know what a revolution is!"). I dropped names like Frantz Fanon and tried to convince a totally heterogeneous group to drop the POC act and help build a better movement. Some observers snapped their fingers with appreciation at the occasional oratorical flourish—and ignored what I said.

I was too frustrated to keep attending the POC meetings. My mistake. There were real ideologues in the bunch, just about four or five of them, but they were vocal enough and fervent enough to drag along the young and uncertain newcomers. The self-appointed leadership decided that a few meetings weren't enough; reborn as the "POC Caucus," they called a special general assembly and announced, in a very unmusical performance, that they were splitting to oppose the racism of the white-led movement against the tuition hikes. A small multiracial crowd watched with some confusion. We couldn't ask them questions or argue with them, because the splitters walked out the door after speaking. I became convinced at this point that I had a personal responsibility to declare publicly, as a "POC," that I opposed this kind of divisiveness and self-indulgence. I stood up again and ranted as I paced in circles, comparing them to the Nation of Islam. I wrote many angry emails to the activist listservs, and commented in one: "I am addressing fellow activists of color: we cannot let reactionary nationalists speak for us, and we need to start reclaiming the legacy of revolutionary antiracist movements."

Many of the core organizers of the Santa Cruz occupation, themselves people of color, quickly recognized that the ideology at work in the split threatened to tie the activist culture to puppetry from above. They wrote a letter responding to the spreading accusation that the occupation, and by extension all organizing on campus, was a "white space." Such rhetoric, the letter pointed out, not only rendered the activists of color who organized the occupation completely invisible, it objectively benefited the administration, which was fond of giving itself exorbitant raises while threatening to increase tuition. If this way of thinking spread, the movement would disintegrate into "collaboration with token POC administrators, who will smile to our faces and stab us in the back." In furious all caps the letter declared: "WE CAN NO LONGER AFFORD TO LET THIS TOXIC CULTURE CHIP AWAY AT THE AUTONOMOUS MOVEMENTS AGAINST THE TUITION HIKES."

Like some kind of world-historical prank, it was just as we were coming to terms with the split that everything came crashing down in Ferguson—when we heard the grand jury decision not to indict Darren Wilson, the white policeman who murdered Michael Brown. It was clear to us that any social movement in the United States, including our own, had to respond to this blatant display of the racism of the criminal justice system. But the latest trends of identity politics made a bridge between issues like police violence and access to higher education functionally impossible.

In the 90s we grew accustomed to the idea that every marginalized identity's claim to recognition must be recognized and respected—a form of discursive etiquette sometimes summed up in the buzzword *intersectionality*, a term originating in legal studies which now has an intellectual function comparable to "abracadabra" or "dialectics." When Kimberlé Crenshaw introduced the term in 1989, it had a precise and delimited meaning. Crenshaw began with an examination of "how courts frame and interpret the stories of Black women plaintiffs." She cited cases in which courts determined that an antidiscrimination lawsuit "must be examined to see if it states a cause of action for race discrimination, sex discrimination, or alternatively either, but not a combination of both." She went on to link this specific legal question to the general problem already described by the Combahee River Collective: that single-issue political frameworks would end up centering the most privileged members of a group, marginalizing those whose identities exposed them to other forms of subordination.[5]

In its campus activist usage, however, "intersectionality" appears to move in the opposite direction, retreating from the coalition-building practices of the CRC and instead generalizing the condition of the plaintiff: equating political practice with the demand of restitution for an injury, inviting the construction of baroque and unnavigable intersections consisting of the litany of different identities to which a given person might belong. Those whose identity is inscribed with the most intersecting lines can claim the status of most injured, and are therefore awarded, in the juridical framework to which politics is now reduced, both discursive and institutional protection. This protected status implies neither the political subjectivity that can come from organizing autonomously, nor the solidarity that is required for coalitions that can engage in successful political action.

Indeed, the immediate reaction to the attempt by student radicals to organize around police violence was to question whether a group which was not black-identified should be even be permitted to address the issue. As a result, black-identified groups staged a couple ephemeral die-ins, while the radical coalition—which included, at a minimum, black, white, Mexican, Puerto Rican, Dominican, Indian, Iranian, and Jewish activists—dwindled in size.

This played out organizationally all over the country, with black separatism and exceptionalism as an assumed starting point. At marches many of us attended in Oakland, the rallies were led by politicians and nonprofit bureaucrats who warned of white "outside agitators" who might try to instigate violence. They said that only black people should take the mic; that only black people should take leadership roles; that black people should be at the front of the march, with white "allies" last and "brown" people allowed in the middle.

"Brown" in this context presumably refers to everyone excluded by the governing categories of "black" and "white." In practice, with our demographic terrain, it encompasses the majority of our immigrant population. Given that, as Marie Gottschalk writes in the *Boston Review*, "the carceral state . . . has dramatically expanded its capacity to apprehend, detain, punish, and deport immigrants," it is hard not to react with some confusion to the suggestion that they can only play a literally secondary role in movements that target the criminal justice system.[6]

The assumption that only black-led organizations could organize around "their" issues, despite the deep political divergences among these organizations—some of which represented the elite interests of a black bourgeoisie and explicitly sought to suppress grassroots militancy—would come to have a deeply damaging effect. Among intellectuals, the most reactionary separatist tendencies were granted the status of a pseudo-philosophy with the ascendance of Frank Wilderson's so-called Afro-pessimism. A fundamental symptom of this trend was the proliferation of the term *antiblackness* in the place of *racism*. The latter, more quotidian term implies an antiracist struggle that unites oppressed groups. The "antiblackness" problematic radicalizes and ontologizes a separatist, black-exceptionalist perspective, rejecting even the minimal gesture toward coalitions implied by the term *people of color*. It claims, on the basis of dubious interpretations of Gramsci and the historiography of slavery, that "blackness" is founded on "social death," the loss of identity and total domination imposed upon slaves at birth—despite the fact that the source of this term, sociologist Orlando Patterson, used it to define all forms of slavery, including nonracialized ones.[7] It follows from Wilderson's reasoning that the whole of "white" civil society is founded on this absolute violence, the entire history of which is reduced to an effect of a purported white enjoyment of black suffering—"as though the chief business of slavery," in the inimitable words of historian Barbara Fields, "were the production of white supremacy rather than the production of cotton, sugar, rice and tobacco."[8]

With ideologies of racial unity functioning as a clear block to the development of mass antagonistic politics, it is no wonder that the seemingly extremist languages of blackness and antiblackness seduced intellectuals into reconciliation with the status quo. Of course, when Afro-pessimist discourse occasionally did discuss the black political class, its tone was one of severe criticism. But this criticism reproduced the political dynamics that led to its rise in the first place: black leaders were castigated for their coalitionism, thus reinforcing the ideology of racial unity that obscured their class positions; their reformist program of bringing black people greater citizenship rights was rejected in language reminiscent of earlier critiques of integration, obscuring the political incorporation of the black elite that has been taking place since the end of segregation.[9] The ideology of blackness in Wilderson's Afro-pessimism functions as a disavowal of the real integration of black elites into "civil society," now hardly a "white" thing. When the lethal effects of white supremacy are exerted by a racially integrated ruling class, blackness as an antipolitical void becomes a convenient subject position for the performance of marginality.

Separatist ideology prevents the construction of unity among the marginalized, the kind of unity that could actually overcome their marginalization. In a 2014 radio interview, Wilderson attacked the view that the experience of black people in Ferguson was in any way comparable to that of

Palestinians. Attributing this view to "right reactionary white civil society and so-called progressive colored civil society," he proclaimed: "That's just bullshit. First, there's no time period in which black policing and slave domination have ever ended. Second, the Arabs and the Jews are as much a part of the black slave trade—the creation of blackness as social death—as anyone else . . . Antiblackness is as important and necessary to the formation of Arab psychic life as it is to the formation of Jewish psychic life." [10]

Listening to Wilderson's bewildering repetitions of neoconservative Orientalist tropes, you wouldn't know that activists in Ferguson had been in close contact with Palestinians, who pointed out that the same tear-gas canisters were being fired at them and shared street-fighting tactics learned from bitter experience. A solidarity statement signed by a range of Palestinian activists and organizations declared: "With a Black Power fist in the air, we salute the people of Ferguson and join in your demands for justice." This solidarity was returned in January when a group of movement activists visited Palestine.

During the peak of the Black Lives Matter movement, Afro-pessimist language spread rapidly on Twitter and Tumblr, encouraging a wide range of activists to describe police violence in terms of the suffering imposed upon "black bodies" and to try to monopolize the very category of death. It was a somewhat stupefying choice of words at a time when black people in Ferguson were constituting part of a global struggle to refuse to accept suffering, to refuse to die. As Robin D. G. Kelley has pointed out,

> reading black experience through trauma can easily slip into thinking of ourselves as victims and objects rather than agents, subjected to centuries of gratuitous violence that have structured and overdetermined our very being. In the argot of our day, "bodies"—vulnerable and threatening bodies—

increasingly stand in for actual people with names, experiences, dreams, and desires.

But in fact, Kelley points out, "what sustained enslaved African people was a *memory of freedom*, dreams of seizing it, and conspiracies to enact it"—a heritage of resistance that is erased by the rhetoric of "black bodies." Furthermore, Kelley argues,

> if we argue that state violence is merely a manifestation of antiblackness because that is what we *see and feel*, we are left with no theory of the state and have no way of understanding racialized police violence in places such as Atlanta and Detroit, where most cops are black, unless we turn to some metaphysical explanation.[11]

Here we get to the crux of the problem. The "metaphysical explanation"—the classic mode of ideological superstition— obscures not only the social relations of the state, but also the contradiction between mass insurgency and the rising black elite that claimed to represent it. Wilderson claims that Afro-pessimism seeks to "destroy the world" rather than build a better one, since the world is irredeemably founded on "anti-blackness." In reality, Afro-pessimism has served as an ideological ballast for the emergent bureaucracies in Ferguson and beyond, since the supposedly radical rhetoric of separatism and the reformism of the elite leadership have converged to foreclose the possibilities of building a mass movement. The "representatives" of the Black Lives Matter movement who got the most media play included the executive director of Saint Louis Teach for America, an organization that has played a driving role in the privatization of education and the assault on teachers' unions. In fact, a group of these "representatives" enthusiastically met with the aggressively pro-charter and pro-testing secretary of education Arne Duncan during his visit to Ferguson—white civil society or not. If such tendencies continue unchecked, the only world that will be destroyed is the one in which poor black students can attend public school or expect to get a job with benefits.

In Santa Cruz, the ideology of identity took us further and further away from a genuinely emancipatory project. Its consequences were not only the demobilization of the movement but also a degrading political parcelization. In the absence of a credible identitarian claim, anti-neoliberal struggles, like the movement against tuition hikes, were artificially separated from "race" issues. "POC" activists would focus on police brutality, ethnic studies, and postcolonial theory; the increasing cost of living, the privatization of education, and job insecurity became "white" issues. I began to realize what a drastic mistake it was when anxious white commentators represented identity politics as an extremist form of opposition to the status quo. This experience showed me that identity politics is, on the contrary, an integral part of the dominant ideology; it makes opposition impossible. We are susceptible to it when we fail to recognize that the racial integration of the ruling class and political elites has irrevocably changed the field of political action.

During a weekend of political discussion among the most dedicated activists, we collectively read and discussed the interview "Black Editor," with John Watson, who explains the organizing function of the League of Revolutionary Black Workers' newspaper. While printing and selling newspapers is no longer an up-to-date tactic, the problem it set out to address seemed quite contemporary:

> As far back as 1960 or 1959 there were people involved in various organizations that were single issue oriented, they had some particular object such as a sit-in campaign, police brutality, war, the peace movement, etc. These organizations had a life of their own—internal organizational activity, with lots of people doing concrete work against the system. But they could not sustain themselves, they would fall apart. Then there

would be a new upsurge, a new organization. There was a wave-like character of the movement, it had its ebb and flow, and because it had single issues it had no clear ideology.[12]

It was impossible to put off the task of rethinking everything, learning how we got here, trying to recover our history, and finding alternate approaches. How could we understand the distance of our contemporary situation from the mass mobilizations of the past when a grassroots movement against racism was being undermined by the very language of antiracism? We organized a study group on the history of antiracist movements, reading selections from a wide swath of historical texts that eventually formed the basis of a *Black Radical Tradition Reader* that spawned reading groups in Oakland, Philadelphia, New York, and elsewhere.[13]

The problem we encountered was that forming a new ideology would have to confront the tenacity of the existing ideology. And "race" is one of the most tenacious ideologies of all.

3

Racial Ideology

Even in the discourses of identity politics that present race as a fixed entity, it is a remarkably difficult category to pin down. One of the most bewildering expressions of its slipperiness is the reaction to people of color who criticize identity politics. I am frequently placed on lists of "white socialists" who fail to take race seriously, for example. Of course, this isn't unique to identity politics. Whites have a tendency to assume that anyone who is interacting with them socially and is "clean" and "articulate," as Joe Biden said of Barack Obama, must also be included in the category of "white." I remember being told by a white person at an Ethiopian bar in Philadelphia that it was disturbing how all the "people of color" were segregated into the other room. It seemed to me that the bar's Ethiopian patrons were perfectly happy to watch soccer undisturbed by patronizing white liberals; I, on the other hand, was rather disturbed that my presence, and the presence of many other friends who were people of color, had been deemed insignificant.

The most disturbing part, of course, is that this whitewashing is not applied consistently. It did not happen when I flew back to JFK Airport on Turkish Airlines and every man with a Muslim name was led by armed guards to an ominous room in the back, where we waited for hours to be interviewed about our travel plans. It has taken me many years to get comfortable with not shaving before every flight.

In social movements, these inconsistent practices are a source not just of personal discomfort but also of organizing errors. I remember a political meeting in which a man rambled about how he didn't "see any brown people in the room." The black comrade and I who were sitting directly across from him looked at each other incredulously.

How is it that a category that identity politics takes to be a fixed essence turns out to be so indeterminate? Indeed, how can something that is absolutely visible and obvious, right before our eyes, still manage to escape our grasp? Althusser pointed out that obviousness is one of the primary features of ideology; when something appears to us to be obvious, like the notion that human beings must compete with each other to gain access to what they need for survival, we know we are in the world of ideology.

There is no intrinsic reason for organizing human beings on the basis of characteristics that ideology tells us are "racial." The ideology of race claims that we can categorize people according to specific physical characteristics, which usually revolve around skin color. But this is an arbitrary form of classification that only has any meaning at all because it has social effects.

Racism equates these social effects of the categorization of people with biological qualities. Such a reduction of human culture to biology is generally rejected and viewed as abhorrent. But it is possible to reject racism while still falling victim to the ideology of race. Taking the category of a race as a given, as a foundation for political analysis, still reproduces this ideology. This is not innocent, because in fact the ideology of race is produced by racism, not the other way around.

There are many instances of the phenomenon of race, and they are all quite different. In order to understand how they operate, we have to talk about these instances in their specificity. Consider the following examples: Spanish settler colonialism and Dutch settler colonialism; English colonialism in India and Japanese colonialism in Korea; ethnic conflict in postcolonial Africa and ethnic conflict in the post-socialist Balkans. All of these examples are caught up with various ideologies of race. But we gain nothing by reducing these concrete instances to a single abstraction, which we then try to explain in isolation from the specific circumstances. As I have already suggested, the better way of proceeding is to recognize that this abstraction of "race" is already an active component of our ways of understanding the world, but to explain it by adding back all the specific, concrete factors that have generated it—moving from our thoughts to the material world and its history.

We also have to break with the presumption that "race" only describes what is different, secondary, and "Other." The primordial form of "race" is the "white race," and we cannot accept it as the neutral, universal standpoint from which a theory of race as "difference" is advanced. In the discourses of identity politics, the category of the white race is rarely theorized because it is instrumentalized as the basis for white privilege. The history of this term is a contradictory one. It is usually associated with white author Peggy McIntosh and her influential article, "White Privilege: Unpacking the Invisible Knapsack." Here, in a well-intentioned attempt to encourage more civilized behavior among whites, we see a clear example of an idealist movement from the concrete to the abstract.

Of course, McIntosh was not the first to try to describe the consequences of whiteness. W.E.B. Du Bois famously wrote of the legal and social advantages granted to whites in *Black Reconstruction*:

> It must be remembered that the white group of laborers, while they received a low wage, were compensated in part by a sort of public and psychological wage. They were given public deference and titles of courtesy because they were white. They were admitted freely with all classes of white people to public functions, public parks, and the best schools. The police were drawn from their ranks, and the courts,

dependent on their votes, treated them with such leniency as to encourage lawlessness. Their vote selected public officials, and while this had small effect upon the economic situation, it had great effect upon their personal treatment and the deference shown them.[1]

However, McIntosh's article operates at a very different register from Du Bois's historical investigation of the class composition of the postbellum United States. This is because McIntosh refers throughout her article, interchangeably, to "my race," "my racial group," and "my skin color." The first "white privilege" she names is: "I can if I wish arrange to be in the company of people of my race most of the time." Another is that she can "go into a music shop and count on finding the music of my race represented."[2]

We will set aside what appears to be a lack of familiarity with the history of American popular music. What is significant is the equation of skin color, the category of "race," and discrete groupings of human beings.

With this equation, white guilt reproduces the founding fiction of race: that there is a biological foundation, expressed in physical phenotypes, for separate groups of human beings who have separate cultures and forms of life. The "white race" as a specific historical formation is obscured by the metaphor of the knapsack.

McIntosh writes: "White privilege is like an invisible weightless knapsack of special provisions, maps, passports, codebooks, visas, clothes, tools and blank checks."[3] The knapsack is carried by an individual navigating an entirely open social field. It contains tools that enable the individual to navigate this field with greater effectiveness than those whose knapsacks are comparatively empty. The resources contained in the knapsack constitute whiteness as privilege, because the knapsack is carried by an individual who belongs to the white identity.

If the knapsack of privileges is carried by an individual already identifiable as white, then whiteness must necessarily be understood as a biological trait. The falseness of this notion is evident: the people who are currently described as white have a wide and complex range of genetic lineages, many of which were previously considered to be separate "races" of their own. As Nell Irvin Painter points out in her revelatory *The History of White People*, "For most of the past centuries— when race really came down to matters of law—educated Americans firmly believed in the existence of more than one European race."[4]

We might conclude that there has only been a minor error of description: in reality, whiteness itself is constituted by the contents of the knapsack. The constitution of whiteness as identity and its constitution as privilege are simultaneous: the knapsack's provisions confer not only advantages but also identity upon its bearer.

But how do we know, then, that the content of the identity conferred has something to do with "whiteness"? Surely, in addition to the specific items conferring a privilege, one would find in any knapsack of identity an infinity of arbitrary details: hair length, gait, dietary preference, computer skills, etc. That is, in order to describe an individual's identity, the knapsack would have to contain everything constituting the this-ness of that particular individual. It would offer us no insight as to the organizing principle that constitutes these traits as something which can be called "white." There would be no way to distinguish "white" characteristics from human ones, Pennsylvanian ones, or heavy-metal ones.

This is the failure of liberal thought. A political formation such as whiteness cannot be explained by starting with an individual's identity—the reduction of politics to the psychology of the self. The starting point will have to be the social structure and its constitutive relations, within which individuals are composed. And it is too often forgotten that decades before McIntosh's knapsack, the term *white privilege* originated with such a theory.

The theory of "white-skin privilege" was advanced by members of an early antirevisionist split-off from the Communist Party USA (the Provisional Organizing Committee), and would come to have an enormous influence on the New Left and the New Communist Movement. A series of essays by Theodore Allen and Noel Ignatiev, collected as the pamphlet *White Blindspot*, offered the initial formulation. Ignatiev and Allen's argument was that the legacy of slavery was the imposition of white supremacy by the ruling class as an instrument of class division and social control. But this was a political theory, not a cultural or moral one, and it held that "white chauvinism" was actually detrimental to white workers, preventing unity with black workers. So fighting against white supremacy was in fact a central part of a political program that favored the self-organization of all workers. Ignatiev argued vehemently that "the ending of white supremacy is not solely a demand of the Negro people, separate from the class demands of the entire working class." It could not be left to black workers to fight against white supremacy as their own "special" issue, while white workers did little more than express sympathy and "fight for their 'own' demands." The fight against white supremacy was central to the class struggle at a fundamental level:

> The ideology of white chauvinism is bourgeois poison aimed primarily at the white workers, utilized as a weapon by the ruling class to subjugate black and white workers. It has its material base in the practice of white supremacy, which is a crime not merely against non-whites but against the entire proletariat. Therefore, its elimination certainly qualifies as one of the class demands of the entire working class. In fact, considering the role that this vile practice has historically played in holding back the struggle of the American working

class, the fight against white supremacy becomes the central
immediate task of the entire working class.[5]

As this language was taken up by the New Left, however, it
went through considerable ideological transformations. The
manifesto, "You Don't Need a Weatherman to Know Which
Way the Wind Blows," circulated at the turbulent Students for
a Democratic Society conference of 1969, proposed a politics
centered on white guilt rather than proletarian unity. The
Weather Underground used the language of "privilege" to
reject the working class as a force for revolutionary change,
writing, "Virtually all of the white working class also has
short-range privileges from imperialism, which are not false
privileges but very real ones which give them an edge of vested
interest and tie them to a certain extent to the imperialists."[6]
In practice, this meant that the Weather Underground equated
political struggle with vanguard groups like itself, who
attacked their own privilege by adopting a revolutionary life-
style. What this amounted to was the self-flagellation (with
explosives) of white radicals, who substituted themselves for
the masses and narcissistically centered attention on themselves instead of the black and Third World movements they
claimed to be supporting—reducing those movements to a
romantic fantasy of violent insurrection. In other words,
the project of black autonomy and self-liberation—which
implied the overall self-liberation of the poor and the working
class—was effectively ignored by the Weather Underground's
race thinking.

Ignatiev ruthlessly attacked the Weatherman problematic
in a paper called "Without a Science of Navigation We Cannot
Sail in Stormy Seas," which is today a jarring discovery:

White supremacy is the real secret of the rule of the bourgeoisie and the hidden cause behind the failure of the labor
movement in this country. White-skin privileges serve only the

bourgeoisie, and precisely for that reason they will not let us escape them, but instead pursue us with them through every hour of our life, no matter where we go. They are poison bait.

This view of white supremacy entailed a very different conception of the politics of white privilege, as Ignatiev elaborated:

> To suggest that the acceptance of white-skin privilege is in the interests of white workers is equivalent to suggesting that swallowing the worm with the hook in it is in the interests of the fish. To argue that repudiating these privileges is a "sacrifice" is to argue that the fish is making a sacrifice when it leaps from the water, flips its tail, shakes its head furiously in every direction and throws the barbed offering.[7]

Today's privilege politics cannot possibly permit a position of this kind. We are instead left with endless variations on the Weatherman position, though without the appeals to armed struggle, bank robberies, and Lenin's theory of imperialism. When contemporary white liberals adapt the Weatherman position, they often end up claiming that a new wave of "pro-white" socialists has arisen to defend the "white working class." But their caricature obscures the important point, made by black revolutionaries throughout American history, that the project of emancipation requires overcoming the ideology of race. Although he characterized the material advantages of whiteness as a "psychological wage," W.E.B. Du Bois did not reduce whiteness to an effect of individual psychology. In fact, immediately preceding the passage on the psychological wage, Du Bois wrote:

> The theory of race was supplemented by a carefully planned and slowly evolved method, which drove such a wedge between the white and black workers that there probably are not today in the world two groups of workers with practically

identical interests who hate and fear each other so deeply and
persistently and who are kept so far apart that neither sees
anything of common interest.[8]

When Du Bois suggested that white and black workers have
"practically identical interests," he was not making an appeal
to some mythical "white working class." Still less was he guilty
of some kind of "class reductionism," which decides in the
abstract that class is more fundamental than race. Of course,
some people really do make this argument—and they play
right into the hands of identitarian liberals, who ask how the
young woman seeking an abortion and the evangelical
protester, the undocumented immigrant and the salaried
worker, can possibly have the same "interests."

But this challenge is afflicted by the same condition it claims
to diagnose. It mistakes the casual description of a shared trait
for a claim about identity. We all have numerous interests that
are related to our identities but also to where we work and
where we live. To say that these different spheres of life inter-
act and intersect is a banal truism which explains neither how
our society is structured and reproduced nor how we might
formulate a strategy to change this structure.

Du Bois was recognizing the lived reality of the working
class, which contains white people and people of color, people
of all genders and sexualities, the employed and the unemployed—a multitude of people irreducible to any single
description. A meaningful common interest between them
does not somehow exist by default. We cannot reduce any
group of people and the multitudes they contain to a single
common interest, as though we were reducing a fraction. A
common interest is constituted by the composition of these
multitudes into a group. This is a process of political practice.

White supremacy is the phenomenon whereby the plurality
of interests of a group of people is reorganized into the fiction
of a white race whose very existence is predicated on the

violent and genocidal history of the oppression of people of color. The self-organized struggles of oppressed people against white supremacy have managed to significantly undermine, though by no means eliminate, this kind of organization.

It was no accident that these struggles ultimately put forward the insight that it was necessary to constitute a common interest through class organization, which extends to an opposition to the whole capitalist system—because it is the structure of the capitalist system that prevents all people who are dispossessed of the means of production, regardless of their identities, from having control over their own lives and thus from pursuing whatever interests they may have, in all their particularity.

This does not mean, however, that a "class reductionist" argument is a viable position. As long as racial solidarity among whites is more powerful than class solidarity across races, both capitalism and whiteness will continue to exist. In the context of American history, the rhetoric of the "white working class" and positivist arguments that class matters more than race reinforce one of the main obstacles to building socialism.

Allen and Ignatiev turned to this question in their further research, inspired by the insights of Du Bois. In the process they presented an exemplary model of a materialist investigation into the ideology of race, one that went from the abstract to the concrete. This work emerged alongside that of Barbara Fields and Karen Fields, David Roediger, and many others as a body of thought devoted to exposing race as a social construct. All of this research, in varying ways, has examined the history of the "white race" in its specificity. The guiding insight that must be drawn from it is that this racial phenomenon is not simply a biological or even cultural attribute of certain "white people": it was produced by white supremacy in a concrete and objective historical process. As Allen put it on the back cover of his extraordinary vernacular history *The*

Invention of the White Race: "When the first Africans arrived in Virginia in 1619, there were no white people there."

At the most immediate level, Allen was pointing to the fact that the word *white* didn't appear in Virginia colonial law until 1691. Of course, this doesn't mean that there was no racism before 1691. Allen's argument was to show that racism was not attached to a concept of the white race. There were ideas of the superiority of European civilization, but this did not correspond to differences in skin color.

The clearest example is that of the Irish, whose racial oppression by the English precedes their racial oppression of Africans by several centuries. Today white nationalists distort this history, attempting to use the racial oppression of the Irish to try to dismiss the history of white supremacy. Yet this example actually demolishes their entire framework. What the example of the Irish illustrates is a form of racial oppression that is not based on skin color and that in fact precedes the very category of whiteness.

Indeed, the early forms of English racial ideology represented the Irish as inferior and subhuman, and this ideology was later repeated word for word to justify both the genocide of Indigenous people in the Americas and the enslavement of Africans. Nor was it only a matter of words: the very practices of settler colonialism, land seizures, and plantation production were established in Ireland. Allen demonstrates this with reference to specific laws:

> If under Anglo-American slavery, "the rape of a female slave was not a crime, but a mere trespass on the master's property," so, in 1278, two Anglo-Normans, brought into court and charged with raping Margaret O'Rorke were found not guilty because "the said Margaret is an Irishwoman." If a law enacted in Virginia in 1723, provided that, "manslaughter of a slave is not punishable," so under Anglo-Norman law it sufficed for acquittal to show that the victim in a slaying was

Irish. Anglo-Norman priests granted absolution on the grounds that it was "no more sin to kill an Irishman than a dog or any other brute."[9]

So racial oppression arises in the Irish case without skin color as its basis. We are forced to ask how we end up with a racial ideology revolving around skin color that represents African people as subhuman and that considers both Irish and English to be part of a unitary "white race."

The historical record quite clearly demonstrates that white supremacy and thus the white race are formed within the American transition to capitalism, specifically because of the centrality of racial slavery. However, we have to resist the temptation, imposed on us by racial ideology, to explain slavery through race. Slavery is not always racial. It existed in ancient Greece and Rome and also in Africa, and was not attached specifically to a racial ideology. Slavery is a form of forced labor characterized by the market exchange of the laborer. But there are various forms of forced labor, and its first form in Virginia was indentured labor, in which a laborer is forced to work for a limited period of time to work off a debt, often with some incentive like land ownership after the end of the term. The first Africans to arrive in Virginia 1619 were put to work as indentured servants, within the same legal category as European indentured servants. In fact, until 1660 all African American laborers, like their European American counterparts, were indentured servants who had limited terms of servitude. There was no legal differentiation based on racial ideology: free African Americans owned property, land, and sometimes indentured servants of their own. There were examples of intermarriage between Europeans and Africans. It was only in the late seventeenth century that the labor force of the American colonies shifted decisively to African slaves who did not have limits on their terms of servitude.

As Painter points out in *The History of White People*, these forms of labor and their transformations are fundamental in understanding how racial ideology comes about:

> Work plays a central part in race talk, because the people who do the work are likely to be figured as inherently deserving the toil and poverty of laboring status. It is still assumed, wrongly, that slavery anywhere in the world must rest on a foundation of racial difference. Time and again, the better classes have concluded that those people deserve their lot; it must be something within them that puts them at the bottom. In modern times, we recognize this kind of reasoning as it relates to black race, but in other times the same logic was applied to people who were white, especially when they were impoverished immigrants seeking work.[10]

"In sum," Painter writes, "before an eighteenth-century boom in the African slave trade, between one-half and two-thirds of all early white immigrants to the British colonies in the Western Hemisphere came as unfree laborers, some 300,000 to 400,000 people."[11] The definitions of whiteness as freedom and blackness as slavery did not yet exist.

It turns out that defining race involves answering some unexpected historical questions: How did some indentured servants come to be forced into bondage for their entire lives rather than a limited term? How did this category of forced labor come to be represented in terms of race? Why did the colonial ruling class come to rely on racial slavery when various other regimes of labor were available?

The first economic boom of the American colonies was in Virginia tobacco production in the 1620s, and it was based on the labor of primarily European indentured servants. African Americans were only about a fifth of the labor force: most forced labor was initially European, and the colonial planter class relied on this forced labor for its economic growth. But they couldn't just rely on European indentured labor because it was based on voluntary migration, and the incentive to participate in a life of brutal labor and die early was not sufficient to generate a consistently growing workforce. As Barbara Fields puts it, "Neither white skin nor English nationality protected servants from the grossest forms of brutality and exploitation. The only degradation they were spared was perpetual enslavement along with their issue in perpetuity, the fate that eventually befell the descendants of Africans."[12]

African Americans, on the other hand, had been forcibly removed from their homelands. So the ruling class began to alter its laws to be able to deny some laborers an end to their terms of servitude, which they were only able to accomplish in the case of African laborers. What really changed everything was Bacon's Rebellion in 1676. This began as a conflict within the elite planter class, directed toward a brutal attack on the Indigenous population. But it also gave rise to a rebellious mob of European and African laborers, who burned down the capital city of Jamestown and forced the governor to flee. The insurrectionary alliance of European and African laborers was a fundamental existential threat to the colonial ruling class, and the possibility of such an alliance among exploited peoples had to be prevented forever.

Here we see a watershed moment in the long and complex process of the invention of the white race as a form of social control. The ruling class shifted its labor force decisively toward African slaves, and thus avoided dealing with the demand of indentured servants for eventual freedom and landownership. It fortified whiteness as a legal category, the basis for denying an end to the term of servitude for African forced labor. By the eighteenth century the Euro-American planter class had entered into a bargain with the Euro-American laboring classes, who were mostly independent subsistence farmers: it exchanged certain social privileges for a cross-class alliance of Euro-Americans to preserve a superexploited African labor force. This Euro-American racial alliance was the best defense of the ruling class against the possibility of a Euro-American and African American working-class alliance. It is at this point, Nell Painter concludes, that we see the "now familiar equation that converts race to black and black to slave."[13]

The invention of the white race further accelerated when the Euro-American ruling class encountered a new problem in the eighteenth century. As the colonial ruling class began to demand its independence from the divinely ordained executives and landed wealth of the English nobility, they made claims for the intrinsic equality of all people and the idea of natural rights. As Barbara Fields puts it:

> Racial ideology supplied the means of explaining slavery to people whose terrain was a republic founded on radical doctrines of liberty and natural rights, and, more important, a republic in which those doctrines seemed to represent accurately the world in which all but a minority lived. Only when the denial of liberty became an anomaly apparent even to the least observant and reflective members of Euro-American society did ideology systematically explain the anomaly.[14]

In other words, the Euro-American ruling class had to advance an ideology of the inferiority of Africans in order to rationalize forced labor, and they had to incorporate European populations into the category of the white race, despite the fact that many of these populations had previously been considered inferior.

This racial ideology developed further as the new American nation encountered the phenomenon of the voluntary migration of free laborers from Europe, many of whom came from populations that were viewed as distinct European races: the Italians, Eastern Europeans, and Jews, but especially the exemplary case of the Irish, whose emigration to the US spiked with the famines of the mid-nineteenth century produced by English colonialism.

The Irish, among the most oppressed and rebellious groups in Europe, were offered the bargain that had protected the American ruling class. Frederick Douglass pointed this out very clearly in 1853, at the anniversary meeting of the American and Foreign Anti-Slavery Society in New York:

> The Irish, who, at home, readily sympathize with the oppressed everywhere, are instantly taught when they step upon our soil to hate and despise the Negro. They are taught to believe that he eats the bread that belongs to them. The cruel lie is told them, that we deprive them of labor and receive the money which would otherwise make its way into their pockets. Sir, the Irish-American will find out his mistake one day.[15]

Douglass had gone to Ireland to avoid being returned to slavery and said he was for the first time in his life treated as an ordinary person, exclaiming in a letter to the abolitionist William Lloyd Garrison, "I breathe, and lo! the chattel becomes a man ... I meet nothing to remind me of my complexion."[16] Of course, this was not because of some intrinsic kindness of the Irish. It was rather because, at this stage in history, there were no white people there. This was clear to Douglass because he arrived during the Great Famine. Writing in his memoirs of the songs sung by slaves on the American plantations, he added: "Nowhere outside of dear old Ireland, in the days of want and famine, have I heard sounds so mournful."[17]

But what Irish immigrants realized after immigrating to the United States is that they could ameliorate their subjugation by joining the club of the white race, as Ignatiev has recounted.[18] They could become members of a "white race" with higher status if they actively supported the continuing enslavement and oppression of African Americans. So the process of becoming white meant that these previous racial categories were abolished and racialized groups like the Irish were progressively incorporated into the white race as a means of fortifying and intensifying the exploitation of black laborers.

It was the great insight of Frederick Douglass to describe this as the Irish-American's mistake. Douglass clearly emphasized the novelty of the very description of people as white: "The word *white* is a modern term in the legislation of this country. It was never used in the better days of the Republic, but has sprung up within the period of our national degeneracy."[19] Let us be clear on what the invention of the white race meant. It meant that Euro-American laborers were prevented from joining with African American laborers in rebellion, through the form of social control imposed by the Euro-American ruling class. In exchange for white-skin privilege, the Euro-American workers accepted white identity and became active agents in the brutal oppression of African American laborers. But they also fundamentally degraded their own conditions of existence. As a consequence of this bargain with their exploiters, they allowed the conditions of the Southern white laborer to become the most impoverished in the nation, and they generated conditions that blocked the development of a viable mass workers' movement.

This is why the struggle against white supremacy has in fact been a struggle for universal emancipation—something that was apparent to African American insurgents. As Barbara Fields points out, these insurgents did not use a notion of race as an explanation for their oppression or their struggles for liberation:

It was not Afro-Americans ... who needed a racial explanation; it was not they who invented themselves as a race. Euro-Americans resolved the contradiction between slavery and liberty by defining Afro-Americans as a race; Afro-Americans resolved the contradiction more straightforwardly by calling for the abolition of slavery. From the era of the

American, French and Haitian revolutions on, they claimed
liberty as theirs by natural right.[20]

However, this was not always recognized by socialist movements. Early American socialists in the late nineteenth and
early twentieth centuries sometimes failed to recognize that
the division between white and black workers prevented all
workers from successfully emancipating themselves. We
should not oversimplify this point or use it to discredit the
whole history of the labor movement. The early socialist
parties were largely composed of immigrants who were often
not yet fully incorporated into the white race, and there were
very significant black socialists—including, for example,
Hubert Harrison, who played an important role in connecting black nationalism to socialism at the beginning of the
twentieth century. The majority of the early American socialists were not racists, and in fact openly and vigorously
opposed racism.

However, most of these early socialist organizations failed
to recognize that there was anything unique about the demands
of black workers. They were also willing to work with craft
unions that discriminated against black workers, and they did
not attempt to recruit black members. Without an analysis of
white supremacy, these socialist organizations did not address
the fact that black workers were often excluded from jobs
available to whites, that they were subjected to racist violence
beyond the workplace, and that they could not expect racist
employers to extend increasing wages to them.

The cost of this indifference to race was that socialism was
always competing for recruitment with whiteness. New
European immigrants were often very radical and prepared to
join militant labor struggles. But they were also being invited
to join the white race. Once again, in the case of the Irish, this
meant finally leaving behind the racial oppression that had
become familiar to them in Europe.

This began to change with the reconfiguration of American socialists into the Communist Party in 1919. By the 1920s the CP had incorporated not only many immigrant socialists but also the clandestine organization called the African Blood Brotherhood, which included many important black Communists, such as Cyril Briggs, Claude McKay, and Harry Haywood. These black Communists were absolutely central to Communist organizing, because they argued that the party would have to directly attack whiteness if it wanted to build a labor movement. As a result of their work, the CP threw itself into antiracist organizing in the late 1920s and early 1930s.

This meant, first of all, placing a heavy emphasis on educating white members to reject white chauvinism, and organizing some of the only interracial social events that were held in the segregated US. The party worked to eliminate the influence of whiteness from the ranks of the party itself. But it also sent its organizers down South and into the black neighborhoods of Northern cities to work on political projects. These included unions for sharecroppers, tenant farmers, miners, and steelworkers; armed defense against lynching; legal defense for black victims of the racist justice system; and movements against unemployment, evictions, and utility shut-offs. Robin D.G. Kelley describes some of these initiatives in *Hammer and Hoe*:

> Representatives of the unemployed councils often dissuaded landlords from evicting their tenants by describing the potential devastation that could occur once an abandoned house became a free-for-all for firewood. When a family's electricity was shut off for nonpayment, activists from the unemployed council frequently used heavy-gauge copper wires as "jumpers" to appropriate electricity from public outlets or other homes. Council members also found ways to reactivate water mains after they had been turned off, though the process was

more complicated than pilfering electricity. And in at least one instance, a group of black women used verbal threats to stop a city employee from turning off one family's water supply.[21]

Unfortunately, the complicated history of political disputes within the CP, along with the state repression of the Communist movement, led to this work being cut short. As an increasingly conservative party leadership distanced itself from the project of black liberation, white chauvinism was on the rise in the CP. It had previously been most effectively combated through mass antiracist organizing: by joining different people and disparate demands in a common struggle. But now that this practice had been abandoned, the party launched what Harry Haywood called a "phony war against white chauvinism."

In Haywood's analysis, this phony war only ended up strengthening the material foundations of white chauvinism, now uprooted from its structural foundations and seen as a free-floating set of ideas. Instead of mass organizing, opposing white chauvinism was now seen as a matter of policing the language of those who were ostensibly comrades, thus strengthening the party bureaucracy and introducing a climate of paranoia and distrust among members. As Haywood wrote:

It was an atmosphere which was conducive to the development of a particularly paternalistic and patronizing form of white chauvinism, as well as to a rise in petty-bourgeois narrow nationalism among blacks. The growth of the nationalist side of this distortion was directly linked to the breakdown of the basic division of labor among communists in relation to the national question. This division of labor, long ago established in our party and the international communist movement, places main responsibility for combating white chauvinism on

the white comrades, with Blacks having main responsibility
for combating narrow nationalist deviations.[22]

In other words, in the absence of mass organizing, racial ideology rushes to the fill the vacuum. And without the political division of labor that Haywood describes, the struggle against racism is reduced to the redress of individual injuries.

Of course, this is why reactions to the critique of identity politics can be so abrasive. When there is no other practical organizational effort to combat racism, any questioning of the framework of identity seems like an attempt to deny the validity of the antiracist struggle. In fact, it goes even deeper than this—questioning racial ideology itself seems to be a denial of the agency of the oppressed. In his landmark book *Against Race*, Paul Gilroy describes how this defensive reaction emerges from the ambivalent relationship oppressed people form with their identities:

> People who have been subordinated by race-thinking and its distinctive social structures (not all of which come tidily color-coded) have for centuries employed the concepts and categories of their rulers, owners, and persecutors to resist the destiny that "race" has allocated to them and to dissent from the lowly value it placed upon their lives. Under the most difficult of conditions and from imperfect materials that they surely would not have selected if they had been able to choose, these oppressed groups have built complex traditions of politics, ethics, identity, and culture.

By classifying these traditions within the categories of "race," their role in the formation of our global modernity has been marginalized, relegated "to the backwaters of the primitive and prepolitical." Claiming and defending these traditions reinforces racial ideology but also provides a form of defense and protection. The experiences of "insult, brutality, and contempt" are "unexpectedly turned into important sources of solidarity, joy, and collective strength." This reversal, as Gilroy goes on to explain, is a powerful factor in the tenacity of racial ideology: "When ideas of racial particularity are inverted in this defensive manner so that they provide sources of pride rather than shame and humiliation, they become difficult to relinquish. For many racialized populations, 'race' and the hard-won, oppositional identities it supports are not to be lightly or prematurely given up."[23] But this dynamic is not only a matter of the conscious self-defense of the oppressed. It is rooted in the unconscious, as ideology always is, and it takes us back to the paradoxical relation between subjectivation and subjection that Judith Butler has shown is so central to ideology and the modern forms of politics. A fundamental aspect of this paradox of the subject, Butler argues, is that it is tied up with a "passionate attachment" to power. This is the kind of attachment that children display toward their parents, who are an arbitrary repressive authority but also the models of selfhood and the first sources of recognition, and therefore the objects of love.

We are constituted as subjects within the individualization that is characteristic of state power; we are activated as political agents through the injuries that are constitutive of our identity. Consequently, our identities attach us to this power in a basic and foundational way. This complicated and unconscious aspect of our political experience is what Butler tries to capture:

> Called by an injurious name, I come into social being, and because I have a certain inevitable attachment to my existence, because a certain narcissism takes hold of any term that confers existence, I am led to embrace the terms that injure me because they constitute me socially. The self-colonizing trajectory of certain forms of identity politics are symptomatic of this paradoxical embrace of the injurious term.[24]

As we try to understand the specific form of passionate attachment to racial identity, we have to pass into the nebulous terrain of the unconscious—the terrain of poetry, fantasy, and illusion.

4

Passing

In the summer of 2015, the definition of race became a national scandal with the case of Rachel Dolezal. An instructor in African American studies at Eastern Washington University and president of the Spokane NAACP, Dolezal, it turned out, was a white woman from Montana passing for black. "I identify as black," she said on the *Today Show*, thus invoking her sovereign right as an individual working within the framework of identity. Though this revelation provoked both bemusement and outrage, the scandal surrounding it revealed the difficulty of elaborating a coherent and consistent critique of her identity claim.

It was as the flourishing industry of social media denunciation turned toward Dolezal that I picked up Philip Roth's *The Human Stain*, which as early as the end of the Clinton era had narrated an inverted scenario. At a class at the fictional Athena College, classics professor Coleman Silk notices that two students on the roster have been missing all semester and asks, "Are they real or are they spooks?" This word, *spooks*, immediately establishes a problem of interpretation: the ghostly presence of absent students, or a racial slur by a callous professor?

As the novel goes on, we learn that Silk is in fact a light-skinned black man who has spent a lifetime passing for white—a "singular act of invention," as Roth put it, which Dolezal later repeated in the opposite direction.[1] In 1990s America it is not Silk's hidden black identity that destroys his life and reputation, but the somehow ontologically irrefutable accusation of antiblack racism. The novel traces a historical passage from the personal costs of segregation to the contradictions of liberal multiculturalism, as they are manifested in the history of Silk's Jim Crow–era transformation and the narrative of his academic downfall.

Indeed, Roth's entire "Newark Trilogy," as Michael Kimmage astutely describes it, which culminates in *The Human Stain*, reveals the historical underpinnings of identity, as personal memories of American history are recounted to and renarrated by Roth's alter ego, the fictional writer Nathan Zuckerman.[2] It shows that there is something beyond our individual experience in our forms of identity: they are imaginary representations of our real conditions, of structural transformations and the political practices that respond to them. Fiction gives us a unique window into this nebulous relation. In the "lived experience" of its characters we see how individuals make sense of sweeping historical changes that are indifferent to their hopes, wishes, and desires.

The arc of the Newark Trilogy follows the rise and decline of the postwar economic boom, and the ideology of American self-making that serves as the foundation for the aspiration of white "ethnics" to mainstream assimilation. In *I Married a Communist*, Roth traces the efforts of Jewish Communists and trade unionists to introduce the ideal of social equality into the American dream—a personal expression of the Popular Front line that "Communism Is Twentieth-Century Americanism." As a direct result of these efforts, Roth underscores, Communists played a leading role in the struggle for black civil rights. But the pursuit of American equality, which Roth admires, is undermined in his narration by obstinate fidelity to a political program, which troubles him, and it is totally wrecked by McCarthyism.

Then there were the sixties. *American Pastoral* had already traced the life of an assimilated Jew, "Swede" Levov, who has achieved the American dream of personal success—and then watches as the Fordist economy that enabled that dream is splintered by urban conflict, the reverberations of segregation and racism, the social costs of extended imperialist war, and the precipitous decline of manufacturing employment. In the absence of the link to a national and popular will to which the Communist Party had once aspired, Swede Levov's daughter's desperate grasp for a politics of social change ends in the dogmatic voluntarism and violence of Weather Underground–style terrorism.

The United States that emerges from this history frames the farcical, depoliticized climate of *The Human Stain*. With the possibility of integrating social equality into American culture destroyed by both political repression and industrial decline, politics is reduced to the anxious performance of authenticity. The policing of personal identity now unites McCarthyism and the residues of the New Left, recalling, in a bizarre historical plot twist, the "phony war" against white supremacy that Harry Haywood identified in a Communist Party cut off from mass struggle. If the "personal is political," it is in the sense that we are left with no practice of politics outside of the fashioning of our own personal identities and surveillance of the identities of others.

Roth's ambivalence—his close attention to the historical reality of segregation and the broad social effects of US postwar economic history, combined with a cynical despair at the depoliticization which followed—leads him to an acute diagnosis of the experience of the present. It cannot, however, be substituted for the kind of historical analysis and political response that the present requires. This dilemma had been illustrated dramatically in 1964, in an acrimonious exchange between Roth and the black poet and militant Amiri Baraka, then still known as LeRoi Jones.

The exchange began with Roth's negative review of Jones's *The Dutchman*, along with James Baldwin's *Blues for Mister Charlie*, in the *New York Review of Books*. *The Dutchman* had presented a theatrical allegory of the failures of liberal integrationism and the seductive treachery of the white world. Roth's dismissive review displays no real understanding of the political critique at work in the play; nevertheless, the line that became the real point of contention contains a kernel of insight. This was Roth's speculation that Baraka/Jones wrote *The Dutchman* for a white audience, "not so that they should be moved to pity or to fear, but to humiliation and self-hatred." Jones retorted in a vicious letter: "The main rot in the minds of 'academic' liberals like yourself, is that you take your own distortion of the world to be somehow more profound than the cracker's."[3]

Like the characters in Roth's novels, the biographies of these two figures and their fictionalized representations of their experience reveal broader processes of social change. The revelation is all the more dramatic since their lives and work revolved around the same city: Newark, New Jersey, a microcosm of US urban and industrial history and the mutations of identity.

Roth, born in Newark just a year before Baraka, had an experience of the city that diverged from Baraka's along predictable lines. Larry Schwartz points out that Roth's youth in the Jewish neighborhood of Weequahic was part of the brief period of respite from the city's long and early industrial decline—which resumed with a vengeance in the 1950s, alongside ongoing black in-migration and white flight. Roth's nostalgia for this period leads to an uncharacteristically naive romanticization of the world, obscuring the racial and class inequalities of the city. As Schwartz puts it, "When imagining the racial politics of Newark, Roth the hard-edged, thoughtful, and ironical realist, becomes a conservative 'utopian'—too much caught up in the interplay between his liberal, civil rights conscience and his sentimentalizing of Weequahic."[4]

However, Roth's own grappling with a New Jersey Jewish identity would subject him to the religious and cultural policing of that community—he was openly attacked as a "self-hating Jew" after the publication of *Goodbye, Columbus*, at a 1962 event alongside Ralph Ellison at Yeshiva University on "the crisis of conscience in minority writers of fiction." He would later reflect in the preface to that book's thirtieth-anniversary edition on the "ambivalence that was to stimulate his imagination": "the desire to repudiate and the desire to cling, a sense of allegiance and the need to rebel, the alluring dream of escaping into the challenging unknown and the counterdream of holding fast to the familiar."[5]

In Roth's case, an inclination toward the kind of social critique that springs from estrangement did not lead in a politicizing direction, but it did lead to a sharp sensitivity to the ideologies of identity, one that fractures his nostalgic selfhood. What his review of *The Dutchman* had captured accurately, in spite of his political evasion, was its author's peculiar relationship to his audience—the whiteness of his audience, the source of LeRoi Jones's inner strife. *The Dutchman* was part of an aesthetic insurrection by Jones against his own white Village environment, and indeed his own internalization of its standards of identity.

However, what Roth had not grasped was that *The Dutchman*, first performed just months before the passing of the 1964 Civil Rights Act, was itself a significant analysis of the relation between identity and politics in that historical moment. The protagonist Clay, a middle-class, quasi-assimilated intellectual, is forced to come to terms with his black identity and overcomes his aspirations to whiteness with a rebellious rage. Yet since his rebellion is individual, Baraka suggests, it cannot succeed; it ends with his murder.

Baraka's own life represented a passage from individual rebellion to collective organization, moving through the identity-based politics of black nationalism to a Marxist universalism. In fact, LeRoi Jones—before he was renamed Ameer Barakat by the Muslim imam Hajj Heshaam Jaaber, who officiated the funeral of Malcolm X, and then had the name Swahilized into Amiri Baraka by Ron Karenga—was mired in identity crisis from the beginning.

His autobiography recalls a childhood marked by a kind of gradient of the black, brown, yellow, and white: "These are some basic colors of my life, in my life. A kind of personal, yet fairly objective class analysis that corresponds (check it) to some real shit out in the streets in these houses and in some people's heads." The "brown" existence of the Jones family in Newark wasn't quite the "yellow" incorporation into white suburban professional life, nor was it the black life of "the damned, the left behind, the left out."[6] With parents who worked in offices and days spent with white students and teachers at school, he experienced class differentiation within the black community in ambivalent, color-coded terms.

It was Jones's education, his training as an intellectual, that would push him toward the lighter end of the gradient. Leaving white, alienating Rutgers, he passed through the brown and yellow world of Howard University, where he came to know the future "black bourgeoisie," both in his social life and in the courses of E. Franklin Frazier. After dropping out and starting an abortive stint in the Air Force, he read intensively and began to develop an interest in becoming a writer. But it proved difficult for Jones to recognize himself in this role. As he recounted, "My reading was, in the main, white people ... So that my ascent toward some ideal intellectual pose was at the same time a trip toward a white-out I couldn't even understand." "White people's words" caught him in a "tangle of nonself": "A nonself creation where you become other than you as you. Where the harnesses of black life are loosened and you free-float, you think, in the great sunkissed intellectual waygonesphere. Imbibing, gobbling, stuffing yourself with reflections of the *other*."[7]

When Jones finally wound up in Greenwich Village, the white-out reached its peak. In an introduction to his 1965 essay collection *Home,* he wrote: "Having been taught that art was 'what white men do,' I almost became one, to have a go at it."[8] Any personal success for Jones as an intellectual thus meant a kind of passing. His early, celebrated poetry is steeped in the experience of a divided self, caught between his experience of racism and his entirely white social circle:

> I am inside someone
> who hates me. I look
> out from his eyes.[9]

But any ambitions to whiteness sat uneasily with his emerging political consciousness. Starting with his 1960 trip to post-revolutionary Cuba, through his arrest at a UN protest over the assassination of Patrice Lumumba, and finally bursting forth with the assassination of Malcolm X, Jones grew more and more unsatisfied with an apolitical art.

As the black political struggle grew in intensity, Jones could no longer maintain his divided self. He came to embrace black separatism and attacked white people in his politics and poetry. In one particularly infamous instance, at an event in the Village after the 1964 Harlem riots, Jones was asked by an earnest audience member if there was a way for white people to help. He replied, "You can help by dying. You are a cancer." When another questioner brought up two white civil rights activists who had recently been murdered by the Klan in Mississippi, Jones dismissed them, declaring, "Those white boys were only seeking to assuage their own leaking consciences."[10]

Baraka would later acknowledge in his autobiography that such remarks were fundamentally hypocritical, since these white activists "were out there on the front lines doing more than I was!" Troubled even then by his political hesitancy, Jones made a decisive break with white bohemia, moving uptown to Harlem in search of a black aesthetic and the black revolution. This search would ultimately lead to a return to a native land—the New Ark, as his hometown would be designated by the nationalist movement he joined there. Reflecting a growing rage against the white hipster New York culture that had absorbed him, the introduction to *Home* foreshadows his move back to Newark: "By the time this book appears, I will be even blacker."[11]

The "blackness" he had begun to pursue in the mid-sixties was not in itself a purely political category; it was just as much a disavowal of LeRoi Jones's whiteness. But it also represented his turn toward a specific political practice: nationalist self-organization. Baraka's beating, arrest, and imprisonment during Newark's 1967 riots, sparked by the police beating of a black cab driver, turned him into a symbol of black militancy. It also caused him to turn radically toward cultural nationalism. In *American Pastoral,* the retired glove manufacturer Lou Levov tries to convince his son to move his factory out of Newark, complaining, "A whole business is going down the drain because that son of a bitch LeRoi Jones, that Peek-A-Boo-Boopy-Do, whatever the hell he calls himself in that goddamn hat."[12]

The urban rebellions, in Newark and beyond, were a political turning point on a national scale. They underscored the persistence of the oppression of black people after the legislative victories of the civil rights movement, as well as their exclusion from postwar affluence. They were an explosive indication that such conditions would not be accepted peacefully.

In this context the nationalist call for racial self-organization appeared to be a viable alternative to the disappointments of integration. Komozi Woodard proposes Baraka as a second model of the development of black consciousness—the first being the exemplary case of Malcolm X's "path of the grass roots to self-transformation and ethical reconstruction."[13] Baraka's was the path of an intellectual who gravitated toward a mass movement. His initial participation in the Beat culture of Greenwich Village reflected a "romantic rejection" of society, which opened the way to a phase of cultural nationalism. This rejection converged politically with the collective, grassroots development of black consciousness to which Malcolm X gave powerful voice. Woodard's brilliant political study of Baraka, *A Nation within a Nation*, shows that this convergence was an organizational phenomenon and not simply a matter of consciousness. "Black nationality formation" was constituted by the processes of economic and political development that built parallel institutions, responding to the exclusion of black people from the core institutions of American society with autonomous forms of self-organization. This process stretches back to Black Arts, which was not only an aesthetic style but also a parallel formation encompassing institutions like theaters, schools, and community art centers— above all the Harlem Black Arts Repertory Theater/School (BARTS). Baraka expanded such practices in Newark with the artistic and community center Spirit House and ultimately the infrastructural initiatives of the Congress of African People (CAP), which extended to housing and consumer cooperatives.

In his classic *Black Awakening in Capitalist America*, Robert Allen notes that "racial integration offers middle-class Negroes the pleasurable prospect of shedding their blackness. But when white society, for whatever reasons, appears to shut the door on integration, the black bourgeoisie responds by adopting a nationalist stance."[14] Such a shift on the part of the black middle class intersected with the spontaneous inclinations toward group solidarity and hostility to white society displayed by the black workers and unemployed who participated in the rebellions. By adopting nationalism, the black middle class could legitimize not only its leadership over these lower economic strata but also programs of economic advancement that would leave these strata behind.

When Baraka visited Ron Karenga's US Organization during a 1967 stay in California, he was deeply impressed. The disciplined character of Karenga's organization vastly outdid his own attempts at building institutions in Harlem and Newark. US's ideology of "Kawaida" was grounded in a "black value system" supposedly derived from African tradition. It was a contrived performance, in essence an attempt at passing for African. Baraka would later criticize it as "the university of false blackness": an incoherent amalgam of hippie counterculture and conservative semifeudal traditions, both drastically distant from the real lives of African Americans[15]:

> Abstract metaphysical shit talking bores
> counter revolutionary, selfish, unserious pseudo
> imitators, red baiters, poets forever in residence
> Black studies pimps in interesting tweed jackets
> Frauds in leopard skin, turbaned hustlers w/ skin
> type rackets, colored capitalists, negro
> exploiters, Afro American Embassy gamers[16]

However, the black value system was an ideological effect of material practices that resonated with the political situation. The Congress of African People, the nationalist organization which Baraka worked to build after the rebellion, tied cultural nationalist ideology to the broad and pragmatic political project of building parallel institutions. CAP's efforts in this regard ranged from schools to housing projects, centered on electoral campaigns that would put black people in positions of local political power.

The ideology of cultural nationalism represented these organizational developments. However, black nationality formation turned out to be a deeply contradictory project. The urban rebellions had already convinced policy makers of the need to avert future conflict through economic intervention, consolidating the legal enfranchisement of blacks won by the civil rights movement. What emerged was an uneasy relationship between black self-organization and the white power structure. In fact, BARTS itself was funded by the antipoverty and antiriot initiative Harlem Youth Opportunities Unlimited, with substantial backing from the Johnson administration.

Furthermore, the real grassroots bases of nationalist formations attracted mainstream politicians, including technocrats like Kenneth Gibson. Baraka's early political career as a nationalist was devoted to the successful campaign to elect Gibson as Newark's first black mayor. Such political alliances fit into the project of building a black united front, CAP's central strategic orientation—a united front which would bring the grassroots base together with black political elites and the black bourgeoisie.

However, the almost paradoxical result of nationalism's political victories was the incorporation of its parallel institutions into a more multicolored mainstream. It's a central part of our cultural memory of the seventies: "We've got Newark, we've got Gary, somebody told me we got LA, and we're working on Atlanta," George Clinton says in Parliament's 1975 single "Chocolate City." This list of cities that had won black mayors starts, not coincidentally, with Baraka's Newark, where he played a central role in Kenneth Gibson's 1970 electoral victory, and Gary, Indiana, where his organization had steered the 1972 National Black Political Convention.

"They still call it the White House, but that's a temporary condition," George Clinton goes on to say. I heard "Chocolate City" in my mind the day Obama was elected; this was a culmination of the move from the margins to the center that began in the seventies and quite decisively marked the end of the period when the ambiguity of nationalist politics could still open toward an antagonism against the power structure. The seventies represented a scrambling of the terms of black politics: the parallel institutions nationalism had mobilized a grassroots base to build were now being incorporated into the state itself, facilitated by a black political leadership that used nationalism to its advantage.

In sum: nationalism did, at one time, appear as a potentially revolutionary ideology. The construction of new parallel institutions mobilized a general antagonism against a social structure based on the systematic exclusion of black people. The possibility of overcoming the marginalization of the black working class provided an objective, albeit tenuous, basis for unity between the intellectual leadership and the grassroots base. But the mainstream incorporation of the parallel institutions, marked by the electoral success of the black elite, demonstrated the capacity of the capitalist state to absorb the nationalist challenge. The lingering ideologies of racial unity left over from the Black Power movement rationalized the top-down control of the black elite, which worked to obscure class differences as it secured its own entry into the mainstream. The black political class ascended in the seventies' context of economic crisis, deindustrialization, and rising unemployment. A politics conceived solely in terms of racial unity precluded any structural challenge to the capitalist imperative to transfer the costs of the economic crisis onto labor. As black politicians facilitated the employers' offensive, they turned against the working-class elements of their popular support.

Baraka experienced this directly in Gibson's Newark. Concluding that Gibson was little more than a neocolonialist, Baraka opened up to Marxism and set about reorienting CAP accordingly. In his poem "History on Wheels," Baraka captures the new effects of the incorporation of black political elites:

> . . . The way the rich blackies showed
> after we marched and built their material

        base, now niggers are left in the middle
        of the panafrikan highway, babbling about
        eternal racism, and divine white supremacy
        a hundred thousand dollar a year oppression
        and now the intellectualization, the militant
        resource of the new class, its historical
        valorization. Between them, john johnson
        and elijah, david rockefeller rests his
        smiling head.[17]

Some years later Baraka would reflect on this experience in a *New York Times* article called "A Radical View of Newark," recalling: "At that time I was a Black Nationalist, a cultural nationalist, who did not understand the reality of class struggle. I thought, and told thousands of people, that black people's struggle was against white people, period." The error, Baraka now recognized, was to have thought that by putting a black man in the place of a white politician, "we would truly be on the road to liberation."[18]

"It is a narrow nationalism that says the white man is the enemy," Baraka told the *Times* in 1974. "We were guilty of that, but it's not scientific at all."[19] His political work now turned toward organizing cab drivers' strikes, rather than building a separatist culture. The nationalist experience had shown Baraka that no straight line could be drawn between identity and politics. At one time, that equation had seemed to make sense; black nationalism presented a political program for a demographic structurally marginalized on the basis of its identity. Grounded in material processes of institution-building, nationalist ideology exalted and affirmed this marginalized identity. But it was precisely the racial integration of the American elite, the diversification of the establishment, that made such an equation definitively impossible.

What could be more convenient for a newly elected black

politician, eager to ingratiate himself with the owners of wealth, than the reduction of politics to identity? Neoliberal policies could be implemented with a nationalist stamp of approval, any criticism easily silenced as a capitulation to white racism. This dynamic, Baraka pointed out, dramatically undermined resistance in Mayor Gibson's Newark,

> a city where a Black Muslim is head of the Board of Education, and collaborates with the capitalists in mashing budget cuts on the people of all nationalities by trying to fire 20 percent of the city's teachers, and cutting art, library services, music and home economics out of the curriculum and condemning the cafeteria workers, security guards and maintenance men, who are on strike now, to wages of $3,000 and $4,000 a year.[20]

At this point the Congress of African People was reborn as the Revolutionary Communist League, which would eventually merge with the League of Revolutionary Struggle, itself the product of a merger between the Chinatown communist group I Wor Kuen and the Chicano August Twenty-Ninth Movement. This communist movement was a cross-racial one, a movement which practiced solidarity as an active principle. After this series of conversions, Baraka's Marxism never wavered. But it was situated in a continually shifting conjuncture. Anticapitalist movements in the 1970s had to respond to a two-pronged assault—the harsh attacks on workers by capitalists who sought to eliminate all barriers to accumulation, and the erasure of any maneuvering room for social-democratic reform. The latter consisted not only in the pro-business allegiances of liberal politicians, but also the consolidation of the organized labor bureaucracy into "business unionism."

Social-movement organizers from the civil rights, antiwar, and feminist movements played a central role in the labor militancy that responded to this assault. New Communist Movement formations organized heavily at workplaces, and some, including Baraka's League of Revolutionary Struggle, had members implanted in factories to develop militant caucuses within unions like the United Auto Workers.[21] But the utter force of crisis and restructuring and the drastic rightward shift of American politics overwhelmed the fragmented left completely. We have still not come to terms with the consequences. As Max Elbaum has shown in his indispensable *Revolution in the Air,* a certain dogmatic catastrophism had prevented communists from formulating a strategy suited to their period.[22] When their assumption that a revolutionary crisis was impending turned out to be false, no new strategy clearly presented itself.

Now that the nationalist moment had waned, along with its organizational forms and strategies, militants were faced with an open question that had plagued the New Communist Movement from the beginning: how could a revolutionary organization be built in the forbidding climate of American politics? Marxism provided a clear account, a class analysis, of this process, its contradictions, and the political tasks which lay ahead; but in the context of capitalist restructuring and the decomposition of the working class and its political institutions, the movement lost its anchor in any organizational alternative.

This political crisis of the New Communist Movement would be overdetermined by semi-nationalist remnants. The blind spots of racial unity persisted past the Marxist turn of Black Power. Even a revolutionary nationalism continues the assumption of a unified black "community" with unified "interests." Despite the harsh lessons of the 1970s, this approach left Baraka and many other black radicals susceptible to subsuming their politics into the minimal program of black politicians in Reagan's America. In the context of this right-wing assault, digging in one's heels in the black united front may have indeed seemed the best way to defend the achievements of the movements of the sixties and seventies. In reality, it meant capitulating to the neutralizing tendencies that had emerged to contain them.

Without any programmatic alternative, many movement veterans invested their hopes in Jesse Jackson's Rainbow Coalition. Baraka had known Jackson since the old days—the latter appeared at a wide range of Black Power events, leading call-response chants of "What time is it?" "It's nation time!" Despite his intense skepticism of Jackson's opportunism, Baraka supported the campaign. His calls for joining this support with a mass mobilization against the Democrats were not heeded, and the capitulation to Jackson turned out to be a severe strategic miscalculation when the latter's efforts ended up lending a rainbow aura of legitimacy to the right wing of the Democratic Party. In the new political context of the 1980s, when unity conceived in racial terms could not possibly lead in a revolutionary direction, subjection to black elites meant following the imperatives of austerity.

Perhaps it's our nostalgia for the mass organizations of the 1960s and 1970s that prevents us from facing our contemporary reality. For intellectuals seeking a way of being political in the absence of such organizations, *passing* is an understandable temptation. Strange as it may seem, Rachel Dolezal could actually be the typical case: she exemplifies the consequences of reducing politics to identity performances, in which positioning oneself as marginal is the recognized procedure of becoming political. Contemporary intellectuals "of color" who substitute identity for politics are repeating LeRoi Jones's initial disavowal of his white milieu and the white selfhood that it fostered. For first-generation college students who feel the daily ambivalence of leaving behind their neighborhoods in favor of upward mobility or faculty who hide their class positions behind their skin tones, identity politics appears as a peculiar intro-jection of white guilt.

Passing, in this sense, is a universal condition. We are all Rachel Dolezal; the infinite regress of "checking your privi-lege" will eventually unmask everyone as inauthentic. No wonder, then, that we are so deeply disturbed by passing—it reveals too much to us about identity; it is the dirty secret of the equation of identity with politics.

This is what Baraka discovered in his passage through cultural nationalism. As he experienced the growing class differentiation in the black community and the incorporation of the black political class, Baraka reached the conclusion that his ideology of identity would no longer suffice. As he reflected in his autobiography, that ideology too was situated within a particular class position; it was the predicament of black intellectuals

> so long whited out, now frantically claiming a "blackness" that in many ways was bogus, a kind of *black bohemianism* that put the middle class again in the position of carping at the black masses to follow the *black* middle class because this black middle class knew how to be black when the black workers did not.[23]

The project Baraka initiated of breaking with identity and moving toward mass organization remains incomplete. In the years to come, the New Communist Movement strained to understand the obstacles against rebuilding mass organiza-tion. Paul Saba, who was affiliated with one of the most sophisticated journals of the movement, *Theoretical Review*, has recently reflected on the inadequacy of the dominant trend in the period "which sought to analyze the rise of Reaganism and neoliberalism through the lens of a rising fascist danger." His comrades found themselves turning instead to "the writ-ings on Thatcherism that were being produced in the UK by

Stuart Hall and others," concluding that "the analyses produced there had direct relevance for understanding what was happening in the US as well."[24] With the progression from Reagan and Thatcher to Clinton and Blair to Trump and May, the parallel remains relevant.

5

Law and Order

The election of Donald Trump in November 2016 was a shock in most quarters of American society. His campaign slogan, "Make America Great Again," was feebly met by Hillary Clinton's contention that "America Is Already Great." But the Democrats themselves were to blame for being so ill prepared. Trump's rise was prefigured by a reactionary wave that preceded him by decades. Its US iteration was manifested by Ronald Reagan, who won the presidency in 1980 with campaign posters reading, "Let's make America great again!" While the US left has yet to come to terms with the sequence that runs from Nixon to Reagan to Bush to Trump, the Jamaican-born British intellectual Stuart Hall devoted a large portion of his career to grappling with the similarly unsettling rise of Margaret Thatcher. Hall, a brilliant theorist of race and identity, was also one of the most astute theorists of state power and class struggle. His analysis of the decomposition and disorganization of the workers' movement and the new political strategy of the ruling class is essential for understanding the changed political field in which identity politics took root.

Hall's work presents us with an interesting problem of comparison. Compared to the United States, the United Kingdom appears to be the site of far more vibrant labor and socialist movements, perhaps today most dramatically represented by the existence of a nationalized healthcare system, consistently dismissed as an impossibility by the supposed left of American mainstream politics. Indeed, the UK has frequently had a nominally socialist party at the head of government, and there is a legacy of militant labor actions whose equivalents in the US seem like ancient history.

Yet in the context of Europe, where in certain cases Communist Party membership numbered in the millions, the UK was frequently seen as an exceptional case—a country that, despite being the *locus classicus* of Karl Marx's analysis of the capitalist mode of production and the site of the first industrial labor movement, was completely politically backward, with the Labour Party unwilling to confront the capitalist system and absorbed in parliamentary opportunism, and the trade unions unable to bridge from sectional demands and disputes to truly mass political organization.[1] So for us the UK represents two different points of comparison: first, in contrast with the US, the relative persistence of its labor and socialist movements; second, much like the US, the failure of these movements to establish a viable mass anticapitalist organization.

Along with colleagues at the Centre for Contemporary Cultural Studies at the University of Birmingham, Hall proposed an analysis of the peculiarities of British politics in the collectively written 1978 book *Policing the Crisis: Mugging, the State, and Law and Order*. This study is well known for its analysis of media representations of crime, which have been profoundly influential in the field of cultural studies, especially since these representations are deeply implicated in the politics of race. But the brilliance of *Policing the Crisis* was to situate racial representations in the political and economic changes accompanying the fading of the fabled "postwar consensus" that had prevailed since 1945, when the Labour Party formed a majority government.

To understand the racial dynamics of the representation of crime, *Policing the Crisis* begins in the period immediately after World War II, when the state took over failing industries, employed a large proportion of labor, regulated demand and employment, assumed responsibility for social welfare, expanded education to meet the requirements of technological development, increased its involvement in media communication, and worked to harmonize international trade. Despite Labour's declared commitment to socialism, this stabilization of the economy did not fundamentally alter the underlying economic system. It was, however, able to build a welfare state on the basis of the unprecedented economic growth of the postwar period and, as *Policing the Crisis* put it, representative democracy developed on the basis of the "augmented role of the state in economic affairs."[2]

But the claim to represent the working class, and the equation of working-class interests with the expansion of the state apparatus, would end up posing new problems as the instability of the global economy reared its head. British participation in the global postwar boom had serious weaknesses, caused by the debilitating effects of the imperial legacy and a creaky industrial infrastructure resistant to innovation. It was no match for sharpening international competition, fluctuations in the profit rate, and growing inflation. Yet the Labour Party had painted itself into a corner, unable to manage the crisis within the existing economic relations while still maintaining its base in an organized and assertive working class. Its role would be to contain working-class struggles, to ensure that workers' demands did not interfere with a favorable climate for investment.

This was what Hall and his colleagues, following Antonio Gramsci and Nicos Poulantzas, called "a crisis of hegemony," a crisis not only of the economy but also of its management, and thus a crisis of the state itself.[3] In such a context, in which working-class struggles seemed to confront the state directly, preserving consent as the primary means of democratic rule—rather than coercion—became a central problem. Consumer society had presented potential resources for a solution; the increasing state use of mass media was directed toward shaping a kind of public consensus and transforming values in accordance with the requirements of capitalist accumulation. But during a crisis of hegemony, consensus can no longer be taken for granted; conventional political and cultural practices are challenged, their contradictions exposed.

At the end of the 1960s, a variety of moral panics bubbled to the surface in advanced capitalist societies. A wide range of phenomena, from protest and counterculture to permissiveness and crime, came to be presented by newscasters and politicians as part of a single, overwhelming threat to the foundations of the social order. In Britain, this threat was simultaneous with an escalation of the class struggle, as workers began to refuse collaboration with the state and the union bureaucracies, and rank-and-file militancy and shop-floor organization displaced the negotiating table. Conservative ideology played an important role in the state's response to this threat, as social control tightened at the end of the 1960s and gave way in the 1970s to the "law-and-order society." Moral panic and economic instability legitimated the state's resort to the use of repression as crisis management, rationalizing and normalizing policing. This campaign also had a less obvious advantage: it lent legitimacy to the state's initiative not only to restrain criminality, but also to discipline the intransigent working class, whose strikes were relentless and powerful.

The specific forms taken by racism in the 1970s UK were firmly embedded in this context. Parallel to these cultural and economic developments was the rise of racist anti-immigrant sentiment, announced by the likes of MP Enoch Powell and the neofascist National Front, in response to the redefinition of British identity by Rastas and rude boys. Hall and his colleagues approached this cultural discord through the perceived rise in violent crime. Media representations of mugging in the 1970s had a particular feature, one that persists today: a deliberate and unyielding association of crime with black youth.

Police had targeted the black population since the early 1970s, but after the political turmoil and economic collapse of the mid-seventies, the black populations concentrated in the inner city were also faced with cuts in welfare, education, and social support. Although the US had never experienced a turn toward social democracy of this kind—at least not since the New Deal, which was not presented in the language of social-ism and did not emerge from the electoral success of socialist parties—the parallels are impossible to miss and were clearly noted in *Policing the Crisis*. The urban rebellions, as we have seen, responded to the same kinds of economic problems and were the basis of profound shifts in black politics.

Indeed, in the UK as in the US, a new sensibility of resist-ance had been emerging in the inner city throughout the 1960s, and what now emerged was an explosive situation: "a sector of the population, already mobilized in terms of black consciousness, was now also the sector most exposed to the accelerating pace of the economic recession." The consequence was "nothing less than the synchronization of the race and the class aspects of the crisis." This synchroni-zation was clearly and concretely manifested in the police. "Policing *the blacks* threatened to mesh with the problem of policing *the poor* and policing the *unemployed*: all three were concentrated in precisely the same urban areas." Fueled by the mass media and the rhetoric of politicians, "policing the blacks" became "synonymous with the wider problem of *policing the crisis*."[4]

Hall and his colleagues took pains to show that this upheaval in the inner cities could not simply be understood as a separate phenomenon from the struggles of factory workers. Of course, the two struggles could be distinguished in impor-tant ways, since they represented two different kinds of political compositions and thus two different organizing strat-egies. In the US, this division in political strategy was most powerfully represented by two organizations: the Black

Panther Party (BPP) and the League of Revolutionary Black Workers (LRBW). While the BPP explicitly grounded itself in the agency of the *lumpenproletariat*—in the streets rather than the factories—the LRBW argued that black workers at the point of production had the greatest revolutionary potential.

The great merit of *Policing the Crisis* was to understand how these two class compositions developed out of a unified structural logic.[5] The black population, in the UK just as in the US, also participated in industrial labor, and black workers played a central role in the destabilizing class struggles of the period. In many of the most pivotal industrial disputes, Hall and his colleagues wrote, "black and white workers have been involved in a common struggle." Nevertheless, black workers were disproportionately represented in unskilled and semiskilled labor and bore the brunt of deskilling and layoffs. The effect of shifting ideological parameters in the crisis of hegemony meant that these divisions could play a destructive political role:

> Although the black and white poor find themselves, objectively, in the same position, they inhabit a world ideologically so structured that each can be made to provide the other with its negative reference group, the "manifest cause" of each other's ill-fortune. As economic circumstances tighten, so the competitive struggle between workers is increased, and a competition structured in terms of race or color distinctions has a great deal of mileage. It is precisely on this nerve that the National Front is playing at the moment, with considerable effect. So the crisis of the working class is reproduced, once again, through the structural mechanisms of racism, as a crisis *within* and *between* the working classes.[6]

In his song "Wat about Di Working Claas," Linton Kwesi Johnson summed up how this dynamic of racial division posed an obstacle to the success of industrial struggles:

Nah badda blame it 'pon the black working class, Mr. Racist
Blame it 'pon the ruling class
Blame it 'pon your capitalist boss
We pay the costs, we suffer the loss

Working-class organization was undermined not only by the ideology of racial division but also by its decomposition through unemployment—and, in everyday experience, unemployment was closely tied up with race. Due to the specific effects of the economic recession on black communities, the black workforce now appeared to be something like an "*ethnically distinct class fraction*—the one *most exposed* to the winds of unemployment."[7]

The difficult task was to understand what kind of political agency could be identified within this recomposed workforce. As black youth were increasingly incorporated into the unemployed reserve army of labor, there could be no question that their objective position was deteriorating. The question was how they came to understand and represent this objective process, and the nature of the subjectivity they formed to resist it. Within the common experience of unemployment, *Policing the Crisis* suggested, "the social content and political meaning of 'worklessness' is being thoroughly transformed from inside."[8] Militancy among black youth was coming not from shop-floor socialization but from this transformation of worklessness. Drawing on the journal *Race Today*, which included figures influenced by C.L.R. James like Linton Kwesi Johnson, Darcus Howe, and Farrukh Dhondy, the authors identified emerging political tendencies within the black community. The new political dynamism was

predicated on the autonomy and self-activity of black groups in struggle; and it identifies the most significant theme of this struggle as the growing "refusal to work" of the black unemployed. The high levels of youthful black unemployment are here reinterpreted as part of a conscious political "refusal to work." This refusal to work is crucial, since it strikes at capital. It means that this sector of the class refuses to enter competition with those already in productive work.[9]

The political agency of the wageless, then, lay in forms of self-help, from "hustling" to the vernacular cultures of mutual support, drawing on the Caribbean legacy that migrants carried with them. While there was no necessary political content to hustling, the American examples of Malcolm X and George Jackson indicated its potential to be the site of development for a revolutionary practice. Wagelessness was redefined on the streets "as a positive rather than as a passive form of struggle; as belonging to a majority rather than a 'marginal' working-class experience, a position thoroughly *filled out* and amplified, culturally and ideologically, and therefore capable of providing the base of a viable class strategy."[10]

Furthermore, since the working class in general was confronting growing unemployment, just as the costs of the crisis were being imposed upon it by the state, these new forms of contestation took on a general significance. Earlier reform victories were being rolled back, and the political power of the working class and its organizations were challenged by an "authoritarian consensus." As this dynamic of erosion and onslaught continued within the crisis, the practices of policing and the media representations of crime were by no means marginal issues but central for working-class politics, posing "the most massive and critical problems of strategy and struggles": "how to prevent a sizeable section of the class from being more or less permanently *criminalized.*"[11] Identifying the new agencies of resistance by the black unemployed and finding a way to join them to the broader class struggle could serve as a basis for responding to the authoritarian consensus, which threatened the working class as a whole.

This analysis, however, came up against a potential limit. Wagelessness and its accompanying forms of organization and consciousness could be understood in two ways. One interpretation saw wagelessness and its autonomous forms of reproduction, including crime, as a form of the refusal of work. But a contrary interpretation, which took on a disturbing salience as the recession deepened, was that

> those blacks, in larger numbers, who are "refusing work" are making a virtue of necessity; there is hardly any work left for young black school-leavers to refuse. As large as is the section who have just found it possible to survive through the hustling life of the street, the numbers of blacks who would take work if they were offered it *is larger*.[12]

No clear solution was available for this dilemma; while existing theories of the *lumpenproletariat* provided useful insights, the deployment of this class category in colonial Africa by the likes of Frantz Fanon did not map onto the conditions of the advanced capitalist metropolis as clearly as the BPP had implied. This tension appeared to be irresolvable in theory, requiring the elaboration of new organizational forms and practices.

It is on the basis of this complex and detailed historical and political analysis that *Policing the Crisis* presents an oft-quoted slogan: "Race is the modality in which class is lived."[13] This should not be interpreted as an idealist description of lived experience of race and class as abstract categories, which can then be applied with abandon to every historical situation. It was rather a materialist analysis of the way that, in this particular historical conjuncture, black members of the working class developed a consciousness of class struggle through the experience of "race," which was itself grounded in the crisis of hegemony. In the specificity of this historical moment, it was "through the modality of race that blacks comprehend, handle and then begin to resist the exploitation which is an objective feature of their class situation."[14]

At the same time, since race was also a structural feature of the capitalist response to class struggle from below, an instrument of division and disorganization, this meant that race could also end up becoming an obstacle to the development of class organization:

> Capital reproduces the class as a whole, structured by race. It dominates the divided class, in part, through those internal divisions which have "racism" as one of their effects. It contains and disables the representative class organizations by confining them, in part, to strategies and struggles which are race-specific, which do not surmount its limits, its barriers. Through race, it continues to defeat the attempts to construct, at the political level, organizations which do in fact adequately represent the class *as a whole*—that is, which represent it against *capitalism, against racism.*[15]

However, the prospect of generating forms of organization that could confront capitalism and racism had a new and formidable opponent. The election of Margaret Thatcher as leader of the opposition in 1975 represented the movement of the radical right from the margins to the center, building on the ideology of law and order to advance a strategy of breaking from the postwar consensus. Class domination would take on new modes, registered principally in "a tilt in the operation of the state away from consent towards the pole of coercion."[16] The moral panic over mugging, then, had played an important role in the state's stabilization. The perception of a rise in crime was "one of the principal forms of ideological consciousness by means of which a 'silent majority' is won over to the support of increasingly coercive measures on the part of the state, and lends its legitimacy to a 'more than usual' exercise of control."[17]

Policing the Crisis had shown how the Labour Party's management of the capitalist crisis had created contradictions that opened space for new right-wing strategies, and how popular consent to authority was coming to be secured by new kinds of ideological struggle. What was now emerging was an antistatist strategy of the right—or rather, one which represented itself as antistatist to win the consent of a disgruntled populace, all the while pursuing a highly centralist approach to governance. The trademark American opposition to "big government" finds antecedents and echoes here.

This strategy functioned by harnessing popular discontent and neutralizing opposition, making use of some elements of popular opinion to fashion a new kind of consent. In 1979, Hall elaborated on the new strategy in an essay called "The Great Moving Right Show." It was originally published in *Marxism Today*, the experimental theoretical journal of the Communist Party of Great Britain, just months before Thatcher's election as prime minister. The roots of her rise, he insisted, lay precisely in the contradictions of Labour's crisis management, which had "effectively disorganized the Left and the working class response to the crisis." Whatever promises may be offered by politicians in periods of prosperity—better healthcare, more jobs, new infrastructure—once these politicians enter into government, they are obliged to manage the capitalist mode of production and secure conditions for growth. In the context of economic crisis, they must necessarily propose solutions that are in the interest of capital and can win its support. Even socialist politicians are not exempt from this requirement, and as long as the underlying structure of capitalism remains unchallenged, they must use their links with the leaderships of the trade unions "not to advance but to *discipline* the class and organizations it represents."

All of this happens through the state, so the ideology of left-of-center politicians, from the Labour Party to the

Democrats, amounts to "a neutral and benevolent interpretation of the role of the state as incarnator of the national interest
above the class struggle." This ideology equates the general
social interest with the expansion of the state, marginalizing
expressions of popular power that lie outside the state's
boundaries, and it uses the enlarged interventionist apparatus
of the state to "manage the capitalist crisis on behalf of capital." The state ends up "inscribed through every feature and
aspect of social life," and the demands of crisis management
turn even a social-democratic state into an agent for capital.[18]

This is the backdrop for the radical right, which operates in
the same space as social democracy and exploits its contradictions. It "takes the elements which are already constructed
into place, dismantles them, reconstitutes them into a new
logic, and articulates the space in a new way, polarizing it to
the Right."[19] It is able to appeal to the mistrust of statism, to
the frustration with the social-democratic management of
capitalist crisis, by advancing a seemingly antistatist neoliberal
agenda. Thatcherism targeted collectivist values, but also the
statism that really had plagued Labour from the beginning—it
took advantage of the distance the reformist leadership had
maintained from its rank and file and demonstrated the very
real irreconcilability between collectivist values and the task of
managing the capitalist crisis.

The remarkable achievement of Thatcherism was its ability to
tie the abstract economic philosophies of Austrian liberalism,
advanced by libertarian heroes Ludwig von Mises and Friedrich
Hayek, to popular sentiments regarding "nation, family, duty,
authority, standards, self-reliance"—powerful ideological motors
in the context of the political mobilization for law and order.
This "rich mix" Hall dubbed "authoritarian populism," and its
ideological maneuvers could not be reduced to mere trickery:

> Its success and effectivity does not lie in its capacity to dupe
> unsuspecting folk but in the way it addresses real problems,

real and lived experiences, real contradictions—and yet is
able to represent them within a logic of discourse which pulls
them systematically into line with policies and class strategies
of the Right.[20]

The strategy was remarkably successful. It succeeded in altering
the political discourse, constructing a bloc of public support
for neoliberal restructuring, and forcing working-class organizations to retreat. The long retreat of the working class came to a
tragic climax in the 1984–85 miners' strike. The fierceness of this
struggle made any discussion emotionally charged. Hall had
been highly critical before the strike of the intense hardship
and risk implied by striking during a period of austerity and
industrial decline, as well as the undemocratic decision to
strike without a ballot. He went on to criticize the mobilization of the miners "as men" within a specific "familial and
masculinist" class identity, which had kept the miners' strike
from "generalizing into a wider social struggle."[21]

Aspects of this analysis were probably true. But it provoked
understandable derision from many on the left. Such a criticism of trade unions in the context of overwhelming capitalist
assault seemed to strike the wrong note. One of Hall's critics
was the sociologist Ralph Miliband, who questioned his
framework in an article called "The New Revisionism in
Britain," published in *New Left Review* in 1985. Miliband's
primary concern was to defend the primacy of class, which he
equated to the central role of organized labor in the socialist
movement—a tune we often hear today. This primacy,
Miliband argued, arose from the fact that "no other group,
movement or force in capitalist society is remotely capable of
mounting as effective and formidable a challenge to the existing structures of power and privilege as it is in the power of
organized labour to mount."[22]

The challenge to this primacy, in Miliband's reading, had
come from what were called the "new social movements": the

movements that emerged outside of organized labor and had demands oriented around race, gender, sexuality, ecology, and other issues not explicitly presented in class terms. Miliband reasonably reminded his readers that "the working class includes very large numbers of people who are also members of 'new social movements,' or who are part of the constituency which these movements seek to reach." But he also argued that it would be a mistake for these people to understand their experiences of oppression through their identities. In fact, the category of "class politics" encompassed the new social movements, since organized labor did not fight for its own "economistic" and "corporate" ends, "but for the whole working class and many beyond it." Though such a struggle "requires a system of popular alliances," Miliband maintained that "it is only the organized working class which can form the basis of that system."[23]

Left unexplained, however, was how the working class would be organized, in the context of the disorganization from above that Thatcherism had pioneered. Miliband's discussion of the new social movements remained speculative, without serious investigation of the questions they raised about the range and variation of working-class experience, the content of working-class demands, and the forms of organization that could arise outside of unions and parties. In contrast, Hall's own analysis of race as a "modality" through which black workers became aware of their class position was based on an analysis of the composition of the black working class, the history of migrant culture, and the political organizations of black struggles—and he was able to build upon this to identify potential forms of political activity with general relevance for the working class as a whole, since racism was part of the way laboring populations were structured by capital.

Paul Gilroy, a doctoral student with Hall at the Centre for Contemporary Cultural Studies during this period, elaborated in his book *There Ain't No Black in the Union Jack* on the challenge this posed both to idealist theories of racism and reductionist theories of class:

> Racism is not a unitary event based on psychological aberration nor some ahistorical antipathy to blacks which is the cultural legacy of empire and which continues to saturate the consciousness of all white Britons regardless of age, gender, income or circumstances. It must be understood as a process. Bringing blacks into history outside the categories of problem and victim, and establishing the historical character of racism in opposition to the idea that it is an eternal or natural phenomenon, depends on a capacity to comprehend political, ideological, and economic change.

So instead of a "platonist answer to the question of where 'races' slide between the world of real relations and the world of phenomenal forms," Gilroy argued, the task of a materialist analysis was to show how "racial meanings, solidarity and identities provide the basis for action":

> Different patterns of "racial" activity and political struggle will appear in determinate historical conditions. They are not conceived as a straightforward alternative to class struggle at the level of economic analysis, but must be recognized to be potentially both an alternative to class consciousness at the political level and as a factor in the contingent processes in which classes themselves are formed.[24]

Miliband's argument seemed to brush these questions aside. He was criticized for this by his wife, Marion Kozak, who thought the "New Revisionism" article "overstated the primacy of class and failed to attach sufficient weight to social movements, viewing them as divisive rather than as potential allies for class-based movements—as, for example, in women's groups supporting the miners."[25] Such unexpected lines of alliance have recently been dramatized in the film *Pride* (2014), which shows the fundraising efforts of Lesbians and Gays Support the Miners (a gesture of solidarity returned by the participation of Welsh miner groups at the 1985 London Pride march) and the National Union of Mineworkers' decisive support for a successful Labour Party resolution in favor of LGBT rights.[26] As Doreen Massey and Hilary Wainwright wrote at the time in their commentary on feminist strike support groups, "It is not a question of either industrial action or the new social movements, nor is it one of just adding the two together ... New institutions can be built through which 'class politics' can be seen as more than simply industrial militancy plus parliamentary representation."[27] It was the urgency of such new institutions, and the difficulty of constructing them, that underlay Hall's pessimism during the miners' strike:

> The strike was thus doomed to be fought and lost as an old rather than as a new form of politics. To those of us who felt this from very early on, it was doubly unbearable because—in the solidarity it displayed, the gigantic levels of support it engendered, the unparalleled involvement of the women in the mining communities, the feminist presence in the strike, the breaking down of barriers between different social interests which it presaged—the miners' strike was in fact instinctually with the politics of the new, it was a major engagement with Thatcherism which should have marked the transition to the politics of the present and future, but which was fought and lost, imprisoned in the categories and strategies of the past.[28]

But if each side of the debate had a point, it is not clear that any participant understood what the catastrophic defeat of the miners' strike truly represented. Despite Hall's account of the powerful effects of authoritarian populism, his theory did not seem to anticipate how drastically this defeat would change the field of political action or how thoroughgoing its consequences it would be.

A major oversight in our understanding of the neoliberal transition is the failure to understand that this moment was also a defeat for the new social movements, just as much as it was for organized labor. While the demands of these movements lived on, they grew increasingly detached from the grassroots mass mobilizations that could advance the demands as a challenge to the whole system. Enormous progress was made at a cultural level, fundamentally changing our language. But the underlying material structures were spared.

As a result, the progressive languages of the new social movements, uprooted from their grassroots base, would be appropriated as a new ruling-class strategy. Bill Clinton, who followed the lead of Thatcher and Reagan and inspired Tony Blair's Thatcherite rebranding of the Labour Party, not only brought us the North American Free Trade Agreement (NAFTA), the Crime Bill, and the Welfare Reform Bill, but also embedded politics in a particular cultural style, driven by focus groups and image consultants, that played on the diversity of the new times—leading Toni Morrison to comment, famously, that Clinton was "the first black president." Yet while Bill played sax on the *Arsenio Hall Show*, Hillary Clinton was describing black youths as "superpredators"—a comment of which Black Lives Matter activists reminded her during her 2016 campaign. A term beyond *authoritarian populism* will probably be needed to describe this phenomenon, which showed, on the one hand, that the hegemonic strategy of the right was so successful as to absorb the putative left and facilitate the consolidation of economic inequality and the further rollback of reforms previously condensed in the state; and, on the other hand, that pluralism, the celebration of the popular media, and the turn to youth culture did not necessarily constitute an oppositional force in the absence of viable revolutionary mobilization—as the grassroots campaigns for the actual first black president would later demonstrate.

It is precisely on the stymied development of an antagonistic agent that the discussion of culture and ideology must be situated—not as an explanation for the complex mechanisms of shifts in electoral politics. Long after Thatcher and Reagan, an industry of commentators continues to ask why working-class Americans vote against their "interests," inviting us to pit Kansas against Connecticut, red state against blue state. But it is in fact in the decomposition and disorganization of the working class that we must seek an explanation for the rise of the right—not in consciousness, false or otherwise. The empirical evidence shows that the US working class, measured by income, has a consistent voting preference for the Democrats, and this holds true even if we restrict our data to the "white working class." But, contrary to the market logic of "interests," this voting practice has never actually increased working-class power, and so the indeterminate ether of American public opinion ends up subordinated to the organizational power of right-wing vanguards.[29]

Whether authoritarian populism has changed people's *ideas* is a poorly framed question. Its role in the neoliberal transformation was to attack the possibility of strategic alliances between the new social movements and organization at the point of production. Traditionalist ideologies of family, church, and nation were a preemptive strike against the potential political barrier to accumulation that these lines of alliance could impose from below. As Paul Gilroy puts it:

> The populist impulse in recent patterns of radicalization is a response to the crisis of representation. The right has created a language of nation which gains populist power from calculated ambiguities that allow it to transmit itself as a language of "race." At the same time, the political resources of the white working class are unable to offer a vision, language or

practice capable of providing an alternative. They are currently unable to represent the class as a class, that is outside the categories in which capital structures and reproduces it by means of "race."[30]

To confront the white identity politics that make up the right-wing populism currently occupying the White House, we need to provide alternative visions, languages, and practices—and responding with a contrary, pluralist identity politics has not been successful. The "renaturalization of capitalism" that Wendy Brown described is precisely a symptom of the defeat and disorganization of mass movements. As Brown commented in a 1999 reflection on Hall and his legacy, the result has been

> a Left that has become more attached to its impossibility than to its potential fruitfulness, a Left that is most at home dwelling not in hopefulness but in its own marginality and failure, a Left that is thus caught in a structure of melancholic attachment to a certain strain of its own dead past, whose spirit is deathly, whose structure of desire is backward-looking and punishing.[31]

This melancholic sensibility is difficult to escape. I am often surprised to hear it even from my undergraduate students, who—between schoolwork and two or three part-time jobs—seem to have run out of time to cultivate a spirit of youthful and rebellious optimism. I have come to think that this sadness is the primary cause of the restriction of politics to one's personal identity. Not only has the idea of universal emancipation come to seem old-fashioned and outmoded, the very possibility of achieving anything beyond the temporary protection of individual comfort seems like a delusion. Hence a call for universally beneficial social change is often heard as a personal affront: instead of an affirmation of my individual demand for security and recognition, I am presented with a goal that lies beyond my powers to achieve. But if we are attentive to the lines of struggle that lie outside the boundaries of the state, universal emancipation appears on the horizon.

6

Universality

As Ronald Reagan was ushering in the era of neoliberalism, my parents immigrated to the United States from Karachi, Pakistan. Hoping to pursue academic careers in an environment of intellectual freedom and material abundance, they settled in the middle of rural Pennsylvania, where there were no mangos in the supermarket.

In a large crowd of demonstrators at San Francisco International Airport in January 2017, I imagined their arrival. As you would expect at an airport, the crowd was diverse: a global array of nationalities, ages, and dispositions. But in the place of exhaustion and anxiety, this crowd displayed energy and outrage. They shouted loudly, against the "Muslim ban" announced by Donald Trump in his first weeks in office, that *refugees are welcome here*. By sheer numbers they managed to shut down all departing flights. Seeing a young boy there who had fashioned a sign for himself reading "Son of a Refugee," I thought of how much my own life had been shaped by the flight that brought my parents to this country. I was reminded of everything the Muslim ban threatened to tear apart—not just families, but the lives and dreams of those who have traveled across an ocean in search of a new life.

Many desires spur immigrants to travel, but they are united by what Sandro Mezzadra calls "the right to escape"[1]: to escape from poverty and persecution, to discover new geographies, and to speak in new languages. The desire of the immigrant is a world with no borders, a world with no detention, a world in which humans move freely and welcome every stranger. It is the recognition that it is possible to think, speak, and live otherwise.

Perhaps precisely for this reason, the immigrant represents a core problem for political thought—not a new one engineered by Trump and his associates, but one as old the nation-state itself. The fundamental contradiction of the nation-state, as Étienne Balibar has pointed out, is the confrontation and reciprocal interaction between two ways of defining the "people." First, *ethnos*: "an imagined community of membership and filiation." Second, *demos*: "the collective subject of representation, decision making, and rights."

The first sense of the "people" internalizes the national border—it is the wall Trump hopes to build inside our heads. It is a feeling of belonging to a "fictive ethnicity," an imaginary community that is constituted by national borders but in reality consists of heterogeneous populations brought together by migration and movement—a plurality suppressed by the fantasy of a unitary racial and spiritual essence.

The second sense of the "people" is the political one, the one that appears to be manifested in our Bill of Rights. It is meant to apply regardless of identity; it is the song of the Statue of Liberty, which offers its freedoms to all the huddled masses yearning to breathe free, indifferent to their particularities.

The contradiction between these two notions is the original sin of the American nation-state. It is stated in the first sentence of its first official document: "We, the People," says the preamble of the Constitution, written by slaveowners. As Balibar puts it:

> This construction also closely associates the democratic universality of human rights ... with particular national belonging. This is why the democratic composition of people in the form of the nation led inevitably to systems of exclusion: the divide between "majorities" and "minorities" and, more profoundly still, between populations considered native

and those considered foreign, heterogeneous, who are racially or culturally stigmatized.[2]

This democratic contradiction came clearly to the surface in the French Revolution, with its Declaration of the Rights of Man and Citizen. In 1843 a young Karl Marx subjected this declaration to critical scrutiny. In "On the Jewish Question," Marx was responding first and foremost to Bruno Bauer's critique of the demand for Jewish emancipation. According to Bauer, any identity, religious or otherwise, was necessarily exclusionary and therefore incompatible with universal emancipation. Demanding the emancipation of the particular identity of the Jew, Bauer argued, reproduced this exclusion, which had been taken to its extreme by the Christian state. Political emancipation would necessarily be universal, and would thus require a kind of disidentification.[3]

But Marx pointed out that secular political emancipation, the separation of church and state in the name of universal rights, had not actually overcome religious superstition in practice. Famously and prophetically, he cited the United States as an example. This was because rights were granted to individuals, Marx argued, and were therefore the rights of "egoistic man, of man separated from other men and from the community."[4] Protecting the individual's rights in the political sphere did not mean the end of oppression by religious authorities and the owners of property. Therefore, neither Bauer's abstract and aristocratic universalism nor the particularism of a minority could lead to real human emancipation. This would involve going beyond political emancipation and overcoming the exploitation of the market.

In an essay on Marx's relevance for the analysis of contemporary identity politics, Wendy Brown summarizes his complex argument:

Historically, rights emerged in modernity both as a vehicle of emancipation from political disenfranchisement or institutionalized servitude and as a means of privileging an emerging bourgeois class within a discourse of formal egalitarianism and universal citizenship. Thus, they emerged both as a means of protection against arbitrary use and abuse by sovereign and social power and as a mode of securing and naturalizing dominant social powers.[5]

This implies a "paradox" for liberalism that persists to this day. When rights are granted to "empty," abstract individuals, they ignore the real, social forms of inequality and oppression that appear to be outside the political sphere. Yet when the particularities of injured identities are brought into the content of rights, Brown points out, they are "more likely to become sites of the production and regulation of identity as injury than vehicles of emancipation."[6] In other words, when the liberal language of rights is used to defend a concrete identity group from injury, physical or verbal, that group ends up defined by its victimhood and individuals end up reduced to their victimized belonging.

Brown shows how this logic undermines the logic behind an influential (albeit controversial) strand of feminism: Catherine MacKinnon's attempt to redress the masculine bias of the law. MacKinnon's antipornography feminism was based on the premise that the right to free speech conflicted with the right of women to be free from sexual subordination. But, as Brown asks, "Does a definition of women as sexual subordination, and the encoding of this definition in law, work to liberate women from sexual subordination, or does it, paradoxically, reinscribe femaleness as sexual violability?"[7] Brown's critique suggests that when rights are demanded by a particular identity group and the whole horizon of politics is the defense of this category, its members end up fixed as victims. Rights themselves end up reduced to a reaction to an injury inflicted on this victim. Their emancipatory content disappears. So by presenting a legal argument that tries to give rights a substantial content, the content of particular identities, MacKinnon ends up producing a fixed and passive category of "woman." The possibility of women organizing themselves against sexual oppression, the kind of organization that implies self-directed mass action, ends up neutralized by a legal discourse.

This is precisely the problem which comes to the forefront in the contemporary "Muslim question." In France, this question was debated in 2004 when the hijab was outlawed in public schools. The question then became: Should the hijab be defended because Muslims are defined by the fact of wearing it? Does the freedom of the French migrant population consist in a defensive response to the injury inflicted by the banning of the headscarf? Surely, the racism implied by the banning of a Muslim accessory should be condemned and attacked. But to the extent that this is framed as a defense of the rights of Muslims, the perspective of liberal tolerance traps the Muslims it claims to defend within a victimized identity rather than joining them in a project of collective emancipation.

As Alain Badiou points out in his book *Ethics*, this liberal paradigm of rights and the defense of victims is the foundation of imperialism, of so-called "humanitarian intervention." The civilizing mission of imperialism, the "white man's burden," claims to defend the mere physical existence of a people. People are reduced to animals, excluded from politics; because they are unable to act politically on their own, they require the protection of a state. "Who cannot see," Badiou asks, "that this ethics which rests on the misery of the world hides, behind its victim-Man, the good-Man, the white-Man?" An intervention conducted "in the name of a civilization requires an initial contempt for the situation as a whole, including its victims." Today's self-congratulatory discourse of moral responsibility and the ethics of military intervention—coming, Badiou points out, "after decades of courageous critiques of colonialism and imperialism"—amounts to little more than a "sordid self-satisfaction in the 'West,' with the insistent argument according to which the misery of the Third World is the result of its own incompetence, its own inanity—in short, of its subhumanity."[8]

Is it possible to go beyond the liberal paradigm of victimhood and the paradox of rights? We have a strong historical basis for doing so if we understand this paradox as the expression of a concrete political antagonism, as Massimiliano Tomba does in his comparison of the two versions of the French Declaration of the Rights of Man. The first Declaration of 1789, Tomba argues, grounds rights in a *juridical universalism*: "the universalism that comes from above and that implies a subject of right who is either passive or a victim who requires protection." Whether it is a woman to be protected from pornographic speech or a Muslim to be protected from religious prejudice, juridical universalism grants no agency to these subjects—their only political existence is mediated by their protection by the state. The 1793 Declaration, in contrast, manifests an *insurgent universality*, one brought onto the historical stage by the slave uprisings of the Haitian Revolution, the intervention of women into the political process that had excluded them, and the demands of the *sans-culottes* for a right to food and life. It "does not presuppose any abstract bearer of rights," Tomba writes, but instead "refers to particular and concrete individuals—women, the poor, and slaves—and their political and social agency." Here we encounter a new paradox: "the universality of these particular and concrete individuals acting in their specific situation is more universal than the juridical universalism of the abstract bearers of rights."[9]

In 1799, the Haitian Revolutionary leader Toussaint L'Ouverture was asked by France to write on the banners of his army, "Brave blacks, remember that the French people alone recognize your liberty and the equality of your rights." He refused, pointing to the slavery that persisted in France's other colonies, and replied in a letter to Bonaparte: "It is not a liberty of circumstance, conceded to us alone, that we want; it is the *absolute adoption* of the principle that no man, born red, black, or white, can be the property of his fellow."[10]

It is still possible to claim the legacy of this insurgent universality, which says that we are not passive victims but active agents of a politics that demands freedom for everyone. It was for this reason that I was struck by the beauty of the crowd at the San Francisco Airport: the decision of so many with no personal stake to defend the rights of every immigrant. Those who had nothing to lose but their own comfort and security were there alongside the children of refugees, shouting just as loudly. They brought into being what Badiou calls an "egalitarian maxim proper to any politics of emancipation."[11] It is a maxim that calls unconditionally for the freedom of those who are not like us. And as any immigrant knows, everyone is not like us, and we are not even like ourselves.

Today it is customary to adopt the language that calls groups designated as foreign or alien "the Other"—a relation that is said to enact a reductive degradation. But as Badiou points out in *Ethics*, the Other is already everywhere, even in you:

> Infinite alterity is quite simply what there is. Any experience at all is the infinite deployment of infinite differences. Even the apparently reflexive experience of myself is by no means the intuition of a unity but a labyrinth of differentiations, and Rimbaud was certainly not wrong when he said: "I am another." There are as many differences, say, between a Chinese peasant and a young Norwegian professional as between myself and anybody at all, including myself.[12]

This seeming paradox was illustrated by a sign one airport protester held that read "Jews Stand with Muslims." The slogan draws on what Judith Butler describes as "Jewish resources for the criticism of state violence, the colonial subjugation of populations, expulsion and dispossession," as well as "Jewish values of cohabitation with the non-Jew that are part of the very ethical substance of diasporic Jewishness." Support for Muslim refugees can claim a foundation in an ethical tradition that is central to Jewish history. Yet advancing a critique of Israeli colonialism, Butler argues, requires rejecting the claim of "the exceptional ethical resources of Jewishness."

There is a fundamental ambivalence here. It is the "significant Jewish tradition affirming modes of justice and equality" in which Butler bases her critique of Zionism. But in doing so, the idea of any one tradition's exceptionality is called into question. To criticize Zionism and affirm justice and equality means going beyond every kind of exceptionalism—it thus "requires the departure from Jewishness as an exclusionary framework for thinking both ethics and politics."[13]

Those of us of Muslim lineage will have to claim our own ambivalence. We might begin by recalling the Pakistani Marxist poet Faiz Ahmad Faiz, who wrote his famous poem "Hum Dekhenge" ("We Shall See") in 1979, in protest of the Islamic dictatorship of Muhammad Zia-ul-Haq. In the tradition of Urdu poetry, Faiz adopted the language of Islam, attacking Zia as an idolater and offering a revolutionary prophecy:

> When the cry rings out
> "I am the Truth"
> The truth that I am
> And that you are too
> All of God's creation will rule
> Which I am
> And you are too

Moving through Islamic language, Faiz was able to point to a politics beyond exceptionalism, a possibility his Marxism provided. We put these politics into practice when we stand alongside others and act according to the egalitarian maxim. I fight for my own liberation precisely because I fight for that of the stranger.

Indeed, those whom liberal thought reduces to passive victims have always been active agents of politics, the source of insurgent universality. In the words of C.L.R. James: "The struggle of the masses for universality did not begin yesterday."[14] Paul Gilroy's groundbreaking book *The Black Atlantic* shows that black radical intellectuals who adopted the heritage of the Enlightenment, as was foreshadowed in the Haitian Revolution, came to articulate a "counterculture of modernity." This was precisely an example of a foundational alterity that is summed up in the word *diaspora* and bridges between the African and Jewish experiences. Diaspora, Gilroy argues, disrupts "the idea of cultural nationalism" and "the overintegrated conceptions of culture which present immutable, ethnic differences as an absolute break in the histories and experiences of 'black' and 'white' people." It forces us to confront a far more difficult and complicated reality: "creolisation, metissage, mestizaje, and hybridity," which, from "the viewpoint of ethnic absolutism," are little more than "a litany of pollution and impurity." But such an ethnic absolutism, Gilroy powerfully shows, obscures the rich cultural legacies that emerge from "processes of cultural mutation and restless (dis)continuity that exceed racial discourse and avoid capture by its agents."[15] Combahee member Demita Frazier has pointed out that this excess beyond identity was at work in the Collective's initial proposal of "identity politics":

> We never actually, as far as I can tell, as far as the classic definition, really practiced what people now call identity politics. Because the centerpiece and the center focus was not an aspect of our identity, but the totality of what it meant to be a Black woman in the diaspora.[16]

However, embracing the radical counterculture of modernity does not mean an uncritical embrace of the European Enlightenment. Gilroy criticizes the celebration of European intellectual history as a manifestation of today's "conservative complacency," which romanticizes the European past and "seeks quietly to reinstate the innocent, unreflexive universalisms—liberal, religious, and ethnocentric." The project of insurgent universality is not advanced by purported Marxists who engage in uncritical and ahistorical celebrations of the Enlightenment, an old and tired position. Gilroy points out that these lazy analyses "remain substantially unaffected by the histories of barbarity which appear to be such a prominent feature of the widening gap between modern experience and modern expectation":

> There is a scant sense, for example, that the universality and rationality of enlightened Europe and America were used to sustain and relocate rather than eradicate an order of racial difference inherited from the premodern era. The figure of Columbus does not appear to complement the standard pairing of Luther and Copernicus that is implicitly used to mark the limits of this particular understanding of modernity. Locke's colonial interests and the effect of the conquest of the Americas on Descartes and Rousseau are simply non-issues.

In such a reading of modernity, not only are the crimes of enlightened Europe erased, so is the centrality of the Black Atlantic:

> In this setting, it is hardly surprising that if it is perceived to be relevant at all, the history of slavery is somehow assigned to blacks. It becomes our special property rather than a part of the ethical and intellectual heritage of the West as a whole. This is only just preferable to the conventional alternative response which views plantation slavery as a premodern

residue that disappears once it is revealed to be fundamentally incompatible with enlightened rationality and capitalist industrial production.[17]

A universal position can only be achieved if we are serious about "reckoning with colonial modernity," if we draw on the Black Atlantic counterculture to put forth what Gilroy calls a "strategic universalism" that goes beyond Europe.[18] Universality does not exist in the abstract, as a prescriptive principle which is mechanically applied to indifferent circumstances. It is created and recreated in the act of insurgency, which does not demand emancipation solely for those who share my identity but for everyone; it says that no one will be enslaved. It equally refuses to freeze the oppressed in a status of victimhood that requires protection from above; it insists that emancipation is self-emancipation.

From the plantation insurrections to the Combahee River Collective, this is a universality that necessarily confronts and opposes capitalism. Anticapitalism is a necessary and indispensable step on this path. As Barbara Smith puts it, invoking a part of the legacy of the Combahee River Collective which must be revived and protected,

> The reason Combahee's Black feminism is so powerful is because it's anticapitalist. One would expect Black feminism to be antiracist and opposed to sexism. Anticapitalism is what gives it the sharpness, the edge, the thoroughness, the revolutionary potential.[19]

C.L.R. James showed that every compromise of *this* kind of universality, every step away from the primacy of insurgency and the revolutionary potential of anticapitalist organization, led back to the particularism of the existing order. This regression could be carried out by any identity, just as the leaders of the Haitian Revolution ultimately imposed wage slavery on the recently emancipated population. As James put it in *The Black Jacobins*:

> Political treachery is not a monopoly of the white race, and this abominable betrayal so soon after the insurrections shows that political leadership is a matter of program, strategy and tactics, and not the color of those who lead it, their oneness of origin with their people, nor the services they have rendered.[20]

In 1957, James met with Martin Luther King Jr. and Coretta Scott King in London, as they traveled home from Ghana. James, in the course of writing his book *Nkrumah and the Ghana Revolution*, listened with great interest to the story of the Montgomery bus boycott in Alabama. He later wrote a letter to King, explaining that he had sent a copy of *The Black Jacobins* to Louis Armstrong and his wife, Lucille, with instructions to send it to King after they had read it. He added: "You will have realised by now that my political frame of reference is not 'non-cooperation,' but I examine every political activity, strategy, and tactic in terms of its success or failure."[21] Elaborating on the meeting in a letter to his comrades in the United States, he summed up what all successful political events had in common: "the always unsuspected power of the mass movement."[22] It was this mass movement that would end legal segregation in the 1960s, establishing a new field of political struggle on which we continue to try to find our way.

Program, strategy, and tactics. Our world is in dire need of a new insurgent universality. We are capable of producing it; we all are, by definition. What we lack is program, strategy, and tactics. If we set the consolations of identity aside, that discussion can begin.

Notes

Introduction

1 Gilles Deleuze, "On the Superiority of Anglo-American Literature," in Gilles Deleuze and Claire Parnet, *Dialogues II*, trans. Hugh Tomlinson and Barbara Habberjam (New York: Columbia University Press, 2007), 36.
2 Hanif Kureishi, "The Road Exactly: Introduction to *My Son the Fanatic*," in *Dreaming and Scheming: Reflections on Writing and Politics* (London: Faber and Faber, 2002), 220.

1 Identity Politics

1 Combahee River Collective, "The Combahee River Collective Statement," in Barbara Smith, ed., *Home Girls* (New Brunswick, NJ: Rutgers University Press, 2000), 268, 264.
2 Combahee River Collective, "Statement," 267.
3 Keeanga-Yamahtta Taylor, ed., *How We Get Free: Black Feminism and the Combahee River Collective* (Chicago: Haymarket, 2017), 59–60.
4 Demita Frazier, "Rethinking Identity Politics," *Sojourner* (September 1995): 12.
5 Salar Mohandesi, "Identity Crisis," *Viewpoint* (March 2017).
6 Michelle Alexander, "Why Hillary Clinton Doesn't Deserve the Black Vote," *Nation* (February 2016).
7 Judith Butler, *The Psychic Life of Power* (Stanford, CA: Stanford University Press, 1997), 100.
8 Butler, *Psychic Life of Power*, 101.
9 Judith Butler, *Gender Trouble: Feminism and the Subversion of Identity* (New York: Routledge, 1999), 189.
10 Ferruccio Gambino, "The Transgression of a Laborer: Malcolm X in the Wilderness of America," *Radical History* (Winter 1993).
11 Malcolm X, *Malcolm X Speaks*, ed. George Breitman (New York: Grove Press, 1990), 69.

12 Philip S. Foner, ed., *The Black Panthers Speak* (Boston: Da Capo Press, 1995), 50.

13 Kathleen Neal Cleaver, "Women, Power, and Revolution," in Kathleen Cleaver and George Katsiaficas, eds., *Liberation, Imagination and the Black Panther Party* (New York: Routledge, 2001), 125.

14 Foner, *Black Panthers Speak*, 51.

15 Nikhil Pal Singh, *Black Is a Country* (Cambridge, MA: Harvard University Press, 2004).

16 Jacquelyn Dowd Hall, "The Long Civil Rights Movement and the Political Uses of the Past," *Journal of American History*, vol. 91, no. 4 (March 2005): 1234.

17 An outstanding account of this history is Geoff Eley, *Forging Democracy* (Oxford: Oxford University Press, 2002).

18 C.L.R. James, "The Revolutionary Answer to the Negro Problem in the United States," in *C.L.R. James on the "Negro Question,"* ed. Scott McLemee (Jackson: University Press of Mississippi, 1996).

19 James Boggs, "The American Revolution" (1963), in *Pages from a Black Radical's Notebook*, ed. Stephen M. Ward (Detroit: Wayne State University Press, 2011), 136–37.

20 Michel Martin, interview with Robin D.G. Kelley, "How 'Communism' Brought Racial Equality to the South," National Public Radio, February 16, 2010.

21 Hall, "Long Civil Rights Movement," 1245.

22 Hall, "Long Civil Rights Movement," 1239–42.

23 Keeanga-Yamahtta Taylor, *From #BlackLivesMatter to Black Liberation* (Chicago: Haymarket Books, 2016), 15, 80.

24 Taylor, *From #BlackLivesMatter*, 80.

25 James Boggs, "Beyond Civil Rights," 367.

26 Wendy Brown, *States of Injury* (Princeton, NJ: Princeton University Press, 1995), 59.

27 Brown, *States of Injury*, 59–60.

28 Brown, *States of Injury*, 61.

29 Kimberly Springer, *Living for the Revolution* (Durham, NC: Duke University Press, 2005), 56.

30 Frazier, "Identity Politics," 13. See also Winifred Breines, *The Trouble Between Us* (New York: Oxford University Press, 2006).

31 Paul Gilroy, *Against Race* (Cambridge, MA: Harvard University Press, 2000), 13.

2 Contradictions Among the People

1 Malcolm X, *Malcolm X Speaks*, 13.
2 George Souvlis and Cornel West, "Black America's Neo-liberal Sleepwalking Is Coming to an End," *openDemocracy* (June 2016).
3 Erin Gray, "When the Streets Run Red: For a 21st Century Anti-Lynching Movement," *Mute* (January 2015).
4 In Taylor, ed., *How We Get Free*, 60.
5 Kimberlé Crenshaw, "Demarginalizing the Intersection of Race and Sex: A Black Feminist Critique of Antidiscrimination Doctrine, Feminist Theory and Antiracist Politics," *University of Chicago Legal Forum*, vol. 1989, no. 1 (1989): 141.
6 Marie Gottschalk, "The Folly of Neoliberal Prison Reform," *Boston Review* (June 2015).
7 See Frank Wilderson III, "Gramsci's Black Marx: Whither the Slave in Civil Society?" *Social Identities*, vol. 9, no. 2 (2003).
8 Karen E. Fields and Barbara J. Fields, *Racecraft* (New York: Verso, 2014), 117.
9 In a radio interview, Wilderson describes the response of Sharpton and the black leadership class as "Black anger management" and coalitions as "an anti-Black formation." *IMIXWHATILIKE!*, "Irreconcilable Anti-Blackness and Police Violence" (October 2014).
10 *IMIXWHATILIKE!*, "Irreconcilable Anti-Blackness."
11 Robin D.G. Kelley, "Black Study, Black Struggle," *Boston Review* (March 2016).
12 John Watson, "Black Editor: An Interview," *Radical America*, vol. 2, no. 4 (July–August 1968): 30–31.
13 Ben Mabie, Erin Gray, and Asad Haider (eds.), *Black Radical Tradition: A Reader* (New York: Verso, forthcoming).

3 Racial Ideology

1 W.E.B. Du Bois, *Black Reconstruction* (New York: Free Press, 1998), 700–701.
2 Peggy McIntosh, "White Privilege: Unpacking the Invisible Knapsack," *Peace and Freedom* (July–August 1989): 10–12.
3 McIntosh, "White Privilege."
4 Nell Irvin Painter, *The History of White People* (New York: W.W. Norton, 2010), ix.
5 Noel Ignatiev and Ted Allen, "The White Blindspot Documents," in Carl Davidson, ed., *Revolutionary Youth and the New Working Class* (Pittsburgh: Changemaker, 2011), 152–53.

6 Karin Asbley, Bill Ayers, Bernardine Dohrn, John Jacobs, Jeff Jones, Gerry Long, Home Machtinger, Jim Mellen, Terry Robbins, Mark Rudd, and Steve Tappis, "You Don't Need a Weatherman to Know Which Way the Wind Blows," *New Left Notes* (June 18, 1969).

7 Noel Ignatiev, "Without a Science of Navigation We Cannot Sail in Stormy Seas," available on marxists.org.

8 Du Bois, *Black Reconstruction*, 700.

9 Theodore W. Allen, *The Invention of the White Race*, vol. 1 (New York: Verso, 2012).

10 Painter, *White People*, xi.

11 Painter, *White People*, 42.

12 Fields and Fields, *Racecraft*, 122.

13 Painter, *White People*, 42.

14 Fields and Fields, *Racecraft*, 141.

15 Frederick Douglass, *Life and Times of Frederick Douglass* (London, 1882), 259.

16 Douglass, *Life and Times*, 211.

17 Douglass, *Life and Times*, 28.

18 Noel Ignatiev, *How the Irish Became White* (New York: Routledge, 1995).

19 Frederick Douglass, "The Kansas-Nebraska Bill" [1854], in *The Life and Writings of Frederick Douglass*, vol. 2, ed. Philip S. Foner (New York: International Publishers, 1950), 317.

20 Fields and Fields, *Racecraft*, 141.

21 Robin D.G. Kelley, *Hammer and Hoe* (Chapel Hill: University of North Carolina Press, 1990), 21.

22 Harry Haywood, *Black Bolshevik* (Chicago: Liberator Press, 1978), 588.

23 Gilroy, *Against Race*, 12.

24 Butler, *Psychic Life of Power*, 104.

4 Passing

1 Philip Roth, *The Human Stain* (New York: Houghton Mifflin, 2000), 345.

2 Michael Kimmage, *In History's Grip* (Stanford, CA: Stanford University Press, 2012).

3 Philip Roth, "Channel X: Two Plays on the Race Conflict," *New York Review of Books* (May 28, 1964).

4 Larry Schwartz, "Roth, Race, and Newark," *Cultural Logic* (2005).

5 Philip Roth, *Goodbye, Columbus* (Boston: Houghton Mifflin, 1989), xiv.

6 Amiri Baraka, *The Autobiography of Leroi Jones* (Chicago: Lawrence Hill Books, 1997), 53–54.
7 Baraka, *Autobiography*, 174.
8 Leroi Jones, *Home* (New York: Akashic Books, 2009), 22.
9 Amiri Baraka, *SOS*, ed. Paul Vangelisti (New York: Grove Press, 2015), 57.
10 Baraka, *Autobiography*, 285.
11 Jones, *Home*, 22.
12 Philip Roth, *American Pastoral* (Boston: Houghton Mifflin, 1997), 164.
13 Komozi Woodard, *A Nation within a Nation* (Chapel Hill: University of North Carolina Press, 1999).
14 Robert Allen, *Black Awakening in Capitalist America* (Trenton, NJ: Africa World Press, 1990).
15 Baraka, *Autobiography*, 463.
16 Amiri Baraka, *Selected Poetry of Amiri Baraka/LeRoi Jones* (New York: William Morrow and Company, 1979), 252–53.
17 Baraka, *SOS*, 160.
18 Amiri Baraka, "A Radical View of Newark," *New York Times* (October 17, 1976).
19 Joseph F. Sullivan, "Baraka Drops 'Racism' for Socialism of Marx," *New York Times* (December 27, 1974).
20 Baraka, "Radical View."
21 See Salar Mohandesi, "Between the Ivory Tower and the Assembly Line," *Viewpoint* (March 2014).
22 Max Elbaum, *Revolution in the Air* (New York: Verso, 2002).
23 Baraka, *Autobiography*, 342.
24 Paul Saba, "Theoretical Practice in the New Communist Movement," *Viewpoint* (August 2015).

5 Law and Order

1 On these themes, see Asad Haider, "Bernstein in Seattle," *Viewpoint* (May 2016).
2 Stuart Hall, Chas Critcher, Tony Jefferson, John Clarke, and Brian Roberts, *Policing the Crisis: Mugging, the State and Law and Order* (Basingstoke: Palgrave Macmillan, 2013), 224.
3 Hall et al., *Policing the Crisis*, 211.
4 Hall et al., *Policing the Crisis*, 326.
5 For an understanding of the complex interrelation of the urban rebellions and factory struggles, see Dan Georgakas and Marvin Surkin, *Detroit: I Do Mind Dying* (Chicago: Haymarket, 2012). The most significant theoretical analysis of this interrelation at the

time was in a 1963 text that was deeply influential on the LRBW: James Boggs, *The American Revolution* (New York: Monthly Review Press, 2009).

6   Hall et al., *Policing the Crisis*, 333.
7   Hall et al., *Policing the Crisis*, 325.
8   Hall et al., *Policing the Crisis*, 349.
9   Hall et al., *Policing the Crisis*, 363.
10 Hall et al., *Policing the Crisis*, 371.
11 Hall et al., *Policing the Crisis*, 382.
12 Hall et al., *Policing the Crisis*, 383.
13 Hall et al., *Policing the Crisis*, 386.
14 Hall et al., *Policing the Crisis*, 340.
15 Hall et al., *Policing the Crisis*, 387.
16 Hall et al., *Policing the Crisis*, 214.
17 Hall et al., *Policing the Crisis*, 218.
18 Stuart Hall, "The Great Moving Right Show," *Marxism Today* (January 1979): 18; see also the more elaborated version in *The Hard Road to Renewal* (London: Verso, 1988), 50–51.
19 Hall, "Great Moving Right Show," 16.
20 Hall, "Great Moving Right Show," 20.
21 Hall, *Hard Road to Renewal*, 203–204.
22 Ralph Miliband, "The New Revisionism in Britain," *New Left Review* I, no. 150 (April 1985): 6.
23 Miliband, "New Revisionism," 26.
24 Paul Gilroy, *There Ain't No Black in the Union Jack* (London: Hutchinson, 1987), 27.
25 Michael Newman, *Ralph Miliband and the Politics of the New Left* (London: Monthly Review Press, 2003), 285–86.
26 See Diarmaid Kelliher, "Solidarity and Sexuality: Lesbians and Gays Support the Miners 1984–5," *History Workshop Journal*, vol., 77, no. 1 (April 1, 2014): 240–62.
27 Doreen Massey and Hilary Wainwright, "Beyond the Coalfields," in *Digging Deeper: Issues in the Miners' Strike*, ed. Huw Beynon (London: Verso, 1985), 168.
28 Hall, *Hard Road to Renewal*, 205.
29 See Larry M. Bartels, "Who's Bitter Now?" *New York Times*, April 17, 2008.
30 Gilroy, *There Ain't No Black*, 29.
31 Wendy Brown, "Resisting Left Melancholy," *Boundary* 2, vol. 26, no. 3 (Autumn 1999): 26.

6 Universality

1 Sandro Mezzadra, "The Right to Escape," *Ephemera*, vol. 4, no. 3 (2004).

2 Étienne Balibar, *We, the People of Europe? Reflections on Transnational Citizenship*, trans. James Swenson (Princeton, NJ: Princeton University Press, 2004), 8. For a complementary analysis specific to the American case, see Singh's *Black Is a Country*.

3 See Massimiliano Tomba's "Exclusiveness and Political Universalism in Bruno Bauer," in *The New Hegelians*, ed. Douglas Moggach, (Cambridge: Cambridge University Press, 2006), and "Emancipation as Therapy: Bauer and Marx on the Jewish Question" in Michael Quante and Amir Mohseni, eds., *Die linken Hegelianer* (Paderborn, Germany: Wilhelm Fink, 2015).

4 Karl Marx, "On the Jewish Question," in *Early Writings*, trans. Rodney Livingstone and Gregor Benton (London: Penguin, 1992 [1843]), 229.

5 Brown, *States of Injury*, 99.

6 Brown, *States of Injury*, 134.

7 Brown, *States of Injury*, 131.

8 Alain Badiou, *Ethics*, trans. Peter Hallward (New York: Verso, 2001), 13.

9 Massimiliano Tomba, "1793: The Neglected Legacy of Insurgent Universality," *History of the Present. A Journal of Critical History*, vol. 5, no. 2 (2015): 111.

10 Victor Schoelcher, *Vie de Toussaint Louverture* (Paris: Editions Karthala, 1982), 264. My translation.

11 Alain Badiou, *Metapolitics*, trans. Jason Barker (New York: Verso, 2005), 149.

12 Badiou, *Ethics*, 25–26.

13 Judith Butler, *Parting Ways: Jewishness and the Critique of Zionism* (New York: Columbia University Press, 2012), 2.

14 C.L.R. James, "Dialectical Materialism and the Fate of Humanity," in *Spheres of Existence* (London: Allison & Busby, 1980), 91.

15 Paul Gilroy, *The Black Atlantic* (New York: Verso, 1993), 2.

16 Taylor, ed., *How We Get Free*, 119–20.

17 Gilroy, *Black Atlantic*, 49.

18 Gilroy, *Against Race*, 96, 71.

19 Taylor, ed., *How We Get Free*, 67.

20 C.L.R. James, *The Black Jacobins* (New York: Vintage, 1989), 106.

21 Martin Luther King Jr., *The Papers of Martin Luther King, Jr., Volume IV*, ed. Clayborne Carson, Susan Carson, Adrienne Clay, Virginia Shadron, and Kieran Taylor (Berkeley: University of California Press, 2000), 150.

22 Sojourner Truth Organization, *Urgent Tasks*, no. 12 (Summer 1981).

Index